*PLATE XV*A. *MISCELLANEOUS EXAMPLES. The stitches used include Trellis, Underside, and Surface Couching.*

SAMPLERS AND STITCHES
A HANDBOOK OF THE EMBROIDERER'S ART

BY MRS ARCHIBALD CHRISTIE
WITH MANY DESIGNS AND OTHER
ILLUSTRATIONS BY THE AUTHOR

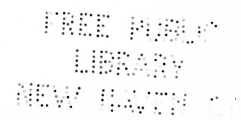

HEARTHSIDE PRESS INC.
PUBLISHERS • GREAT NECK, NEW YORK 11021

Here practise and invention may be free.
And as a squirrel skips from tree to tree,
So maids may (from their mistresse or their mother)
Learne to leave one worke, and to learne another.
For here they may make choice of which is which,
And skip from worke to worke, from stitch to stitch,
Until, in time, delightful practise shall
(With profit) make them perfect in them all.
Thus hoping that these workes may have this guide
To serve for ornament, and not for pride :
To cherish vertue, banish idlenesse,
For these ends, may this booke have good successe.'

JOHN TAYLOR, ' The Needle's Excellency.'

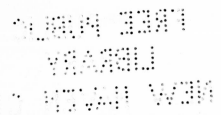

AMERICAN PUBLICATION 1971 BY HEARTHSIDE PRESS INC.
Library of Congress Catalog Card Number 73-151461
(Originally published in England by B. T. Batsford Ltd.)

PREFACE TO THE FIRST EDITION

*T*HERE *are many who would gladly recall, if they could, the past beauties of the delicate art of embroidery, but unfortunately the traditional receipts for the stitches and methods of work, which it used to be the practice to hand down from mother to daughter, are fast passing away. So it seems desirable, especially in times like the present, that these should be collected and placed on record, and in some measure be brought up to date. To attempt this is one of the objects of this book. Also it is hoped to add to the worker's knowledge of materials and technique, because this forms the proper basis of embroidery design. The stitches and methods of work brought together here have been collected for the most part from actual embroideries. These have been classified and presented to the reader by means of working diagrams which often show several stages of each stitch, and a series of samplers illustrate some of the uses to which they can be applied when learnt. In the art of embroidery, the question of design is so interwoven with that of technique that pattern planning, if approached in the right way, grows almost unconsciously out of the study of stitches. It will be found upon experiment that many stitches can introduce new ideas for design. The worker is urged, when thinking over a new piece of work, either simple or complex, to take some characteristic stitches and see what can be done with them, rather than to make a design with pencil and brush and then see what stitches can be adapted to working it out. The former method is fairly certain to result in a true embroidery design ; the latter sometimes looks as if it had been stitched with difficulty, and would perhaps have been better if painted with the brush. Although the study of old work forms the basis of the research which has made up the book, the illustration of ancient examples does not take much space in it, for it is hoped that the power obtained through a wide knowledge of technique should and will, naturally express the changes of fashion which time brings about. The aim is a text book, not of ancient, but of modern embroidery and design.*

GRACE CHRISTIE.

INGLEBOROUGH HOUSE,
  EAST RUNTON, NORFOLK.
    October 1, 1920.

CONTENTS

*G*RATEFUL *acknowledgment is due to Messrs. Jas. Pearsall &
Co., and to the Editors of the ' Burlington Magazine,' for
kind permission to use again some drawings which were originally
made for publications and articles I undertook for them : to Mrs.
Newall, of Fisherton-de-la-Mere, for permission to reproduce
Plate XXII : and to my pupils at the Royal College of Art for
the experience gained in the happy hours we have spent together
in the study of embroidery. I must especially thank Miss D.
Billington, Miss B. N. Morford, Miss D. Moxon, and Miss D.
Taylor for the loan of Plates V, XIX, XI, XXIII, and XXVI,
worked in their college days. The rest of the plates are my
own, and have been worked either by me or under my personal
direction.*

SAMPLERS AND STITCHES

CHAPTER I—INTRODUCTORY

WITHOUT stitches there could be no art of embroidery. They are the means by which fanciful ideas and memories of pleasant things can be figured upon fabrics. In studying the expression of these by the needle's art the first matters to be dealt with are fabric, thread, and stitch. If close attention is not paid to these no great progress can be made, for materials and technique are the basis not only of good workmanship but are also closely bound up with design. A knowledge of the wonderful technique which has throughout past centuries gathered round this art is indispensable to the serious worker. She must have a store of stitch knowledge from which to choose the exact stitch needed, for a good design can be marred by a wrong method of execution. A stitch should be chosen for use because it expresses perfectly the subject to be embroidered. There are used in designing certain elements peculiar to art which have no relationship to nature, and others which are more or less pictorial representation of natural form. Perfect expression of the first type is easy, but success in using elements of the second type depends to some extent upon imitative skill. A representation of a pansy must recall a pansy or it fails in its purpose, but perfect artistic expression is not attained by absolute imitation. However pleasing exact imitation may be it is not a high form of art : it is a mistake in embroidery, as in all decorative art, to be realistic. To absorb and transform the real is the true function of art. The avoidance of realism is a question of design as well as of technique, for the two cannot but go hand in hand. Naturalistic treatment of floral designs is best avoided by the worker with the needle ; there is a place for nature and one for art, and when nature is adapted to artistic uses it needs a certain formalism to make it suit its artificial environment. To give an instance, flowers may be put on the table in vases, they are also pleasing if laid on the table as decoration, but they must not be incorporated with the table linen by means of needle and thread—that is, embroidered upon it—with any pretence that they are real flowers.   Here are wanted embroidered flowers, birds, or other objects, possessing the character and likeness of the thing represented, but in no way trying to make believe they are real, or anything else but needlework.   There are many ways of treating subjects in a satisfactory embroidery manner ; an example of a slightly formalised treatment of flowers is seen in the head-piece above and an enlargement of the same design is shown opposite.   Sometimes workers try deliberately to make an embroidery appear like a painting, and with this object they disguise the stitches by making them imitate the technique of the brush. The technique of embroidery, rather than being disguised, needs emphasising, for rightly chosen and properly used it has much intrinsic value.   Stitches, apart from what they express, possess qualities such as beauty of form, ingenuity and mystery, for they are sometimes curiously wrought, and in this there is charm.   As a rule not enough is made of texture in embroidered work.   By the aid of stitches a monotonous surface can be transformed at will into a richly varied one. The technique of the needle is so naïve and delightful that it can afford to be daring.   By its aid the embroiderer can represent nature or anything else with a combination of fact and fantasy that is most captivating.   In the thirteenth century, when the vestments of priests were covered with fine needle work, a common design for a cope was to decorate its surface with tier upon tier of architectural arcading and to place within each arch a needle-worked picture.   Such a composition may sound strange, yet the result was not incongruous ; one reason why it was so successful being that the subject was not realistically treated.   The artist instead of attempting to represent actual marble pillars, capitals and vaulting, fantastically suggested them by such devices as intertwined branches of columbine or oak curiously worked in gold, bearing acorns of seed pearls.   The capitals at times would be represented by gaily coloured birds within octagons.   Neither were the picture-subjects naturalistic in their treatment.

Embroidery design has much in common with that for other crafts, as certain limitations are common to all decorative work.   These instead of forming obstacles are an aid to progress, they are sign-posts which point out the way to success.   The chief limitations of the art of embroidery are stitch and material, but used in the right way these are so full of suggestion for design that limitation is hardly the word by which to describe them.   When considering a new piece of work it is a good plan to have a sampler of stitches to look at and a knowledge, if not actual patterns, of possible fabrics for the background and of threads with which to work.   For as embroidery design depends largely upon stitch and method for its right expression, so stitch and method in their turn depend for perfect workmanship upon suitable thread and fabric.   Threads vary greatly, they can be wiry, pliable, glossy or dull, twisted, hard or soft, and a stitch may completely fail in effect unless carried out with the right thread.   The fabric chosen for the ground should be of real aid in attaining the result.   It might almost be laid down as a maxim that the more the ground material actually helps to work the pattern, the more pleasing the composition will be. When the stitches are executed by the counted threads of the ground fabric, as, say, in canvas or drawn work, it may be said that both are working together. This interdependence of fabric and stitch is a quality that

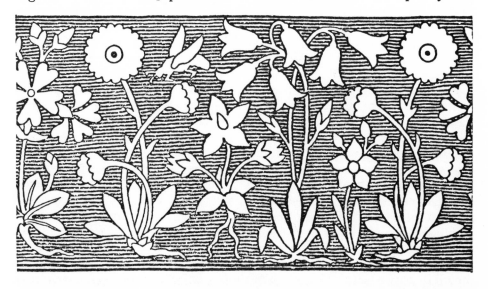

ENLARGED DRAWING OF HEAD PIECE TO CHAPTER I.

traditional peasant work often possesses and upon which rests much of its charm. Again ground fabric aids pattern by being exactly the right tone and texture. The tones of unbleached linens make more sympathetic grounds than the chemically whitened kinds and loosely woven textures, though more difficult to manipulate, look the best. These qualities are well attained in hand-woven fabrics which should be used when procurable, for machine-made and hand-made work rarely weld perfectly together. The samplers illustrated in this book exhibit a variety of possible fabrics for different purposes.

Before starting forth upon the adventure of making a design, it is necessary to be able to draw. Embroidering entails drawing with the needle, a more difficult task than drawing with the pencil, so if a worker has learnt the one, the other will be a simpler task to master. Lessons in drawing and stitching can be commenced at the same time for each will help the other, and there is no reason why lessons in designing should not start with them. For simple work, such as many wish to do, a little drawing helped out by tracing is sufficient. It is more important to cultivate a right instinct for decoration than to take drawing very far, though the more knowledge the student has of both subjects the better. The flowers decorating the band shown on page 3 were taken from a herbal and needed only slight adjustment to make them take their places fitly along the band. The task of arranging a simple design such as this could be attempted by the veriest beginner, for all that is required for it is the taste to choose suitable flowers and some feeling for appropriate arrangement—in this case just even distribution over the surface. The flowers could be drawn from nature, or, if drawing was an insuperable obstacle, they might be traced from a herbal. It is a pity not to attempt planning designs, for if a worker does not make her own patterns the chance of a great deal of pleasure is lost, moreover craft work loses its individuality and vitality if only copied work is produced.

A good way for a beginner to commence the study of stitching, designing, and drawing, is to plan and work a sampler. Usually the aim of a sampler is to be useful for after reference. The elements of which it is composed should be arranged with sufficient order and design to make it pleasing to look upon, to be an object worthy to be framed and hung upon a wall. From the useful point of view it can be a record of stitches and ways of using them. This is accomplished by working rows of stitches in line, which, in a panel below, can be applied to suitable objects such as birds, flower sprigs, or geometrical figures. The sampler should also be a record of patterns and colour schemes ; fragments of these may be a sufficient reminder. It can contain a motley collection of useful elements gleaned from many sources. An alphabet should have a place upon it, for sometimes verses have to be worked or linen needs to be marked. A sampler is more individual and attractive if it reflects the personal taste of the worker, who should be the one to decide what is to be put upon it. It may be the sea and ships, soldiers, guns and aeroplanes, birds, butterflies and flowers, animals, knots, shields of arms, the present fashion in dress, or passing events, or perhaps it will picture a story. (Plates XIX, XXIII.) Let some of these subjects be carried out in appropriate stitches having first been arranged upon paper with due thought for balance and seemliness. Having worked a sampler somewhat on these lines, the beginner has learnt something of stitching, drawing, and designing, and has probably become interested, possibly even enthusiastic, over this creation of her own. If at this stage such

PLATE II. DETAIL FROM THE CENTRAL PART OF A HANGING. Stitches: Rosettes in Interlacing, Striped Woven Band, and Faggot; Surrounding Knot Work in Couched Fine Tape, with Fillings in Faggot Stitch, coloured alternately Green and Blue.

PLATE III. A COLLECTION OF PATTERNS FROM EARLY ENGLISH SAMPLERS.
Satin stitch worked by the counted threads of the ground fabric. Wheels in Buttonhole.

feeling has been aroused right progress is being made. The only things that a pupil can be taught are such matters as technical manipulation, certain principles of the arrangement of designs, and possible elements or units with which to compose them. And if whilst gaining an elementary knowledge of these, real interest has been quickened, the worker is on the right road to develop inherent capacity. In allowing a beginner to put upon her sampler what she is attracted towards, she is guided by her own individuality as well as by the direction of another mind, which is the best way to learn.

Designs are composed of elements or units. These by variation of pose and arrangement build up different types of pattern. For embroidery designs some of the commonly chosen elements are flowers, foliage, figures, birds and animals, geometrical forms such as knots, strapwork, and quatrefoils. The worker should make studies of elements both from nature and from art. Sometimes they are found upon the designs of other craft work, such as pottery or weaving, coming from our own or far countries ; Persia and India have provided us with a wealth of examples of embroidered flowers. Patterns are composed by arranging elements on some fundamental plan, such as repetition, symmetry, radiation, and so forth. The discovery of all this kind of thing—fundamental bases of patterns, main types of border designs, suitable elements—does not come by inspiration but by systematic study. A set of exercises must be undertaken which might be called experiments in pattern planning. These may be carried out by ringing all the possible changes on one idea, by working with fixed elements under given conditions, and exhausting all the possibilities of each case. Having tried a number of different plans, the most attractive and suitable to the particular purpose may be adopted. It is of little use sitting down before a blank sheet of paper waiting for inspiration. The wiser plan is to get together a great deal of experience by tackling direct problems and to look around and see how others, in past and present times, have mastered them.

An embroidery notebook is a useful and fascinating possession ; it should be the complement of the sampler. It can contain diagrams of the working stages of stitches, as a useful reminder, for the sampler will show only the finished product. All kinds of odd, interesting matter can be collected and noted in it, such as studies of flowers from nature, from herbals and other embroideries, jottings of patterns, notes on historical work and many other things for future reference. If the contents of this notebook are neatly drawn and set upon its pages with some thought for decorative effect the embroidery notebook becomes as interesting and valuable a possession as a well-designed and worked sampler.

When the student has practised the making of patterns, and how to stitch them deftly, and has an intimate acquaintance with the many lovely threads and fabrics which henceforth she will handle constantly in the exercise of her craft, she will be fit to undertake almost any embroidery problem which presents itself. For the experience gained in acquiring this knowledge will mould her taste and help to give the embroidery touch to her finger-tips. Taste, true feeling, is simultaneously born in the fingers and felt in the brain. The first consideration, when commencing a piece of work, must be—to what purpose is the finished product to be put—for this question should govern the whole conception. The art of the needle can enter into every phase of life, and add interest to it. In the service of the Church it can ennoble the fabric which clothes the altar, and the vestment of the priest. This branch of art calls for the finest materials, the greatest dignity in design, and the most skilled craftsmanship. In Church embroidery we have the incentive of a great tradition, for England in the Middle Ages was famous throughout Europe for her broidered vestments. Often in Church inventories, after the mention of a cope, as a statement of its value would come the words ' *façon d'Angleterre* ' or ' *de opere Anglico*.' Bishops, noblemen, and kings on the continent vied with each other to procure this famous ' English work.' Pope Innocent IV sent emissaries to England to collect vestments for his choir ' no matter what the cost might be.'

Civic functions may in the future give rise to new developments in embroidery. Why should not our mayors, magistrates, and masters of colleges have their gowns stitched over with symbols of office ? Opportunity for the use of bold types of design and workmanship are afforded by banners and street hangings. Symbolical figures, mottoes, and heraldry, executed perhaps in applied or inlaid work, make suitable decoration for these.

Wearing apparel provides a fine field for the display of the art of the needle. Elaborate dress embroidery can only be discussed by a professional dressmaker, for the embroidery is here secondary to the art of dress. But dainty borders, a flowered vest, or a child's frock can be successfully attempted by the amateur. Simple dress decoration is usually satisfactory if constructional—a neat insertion joining a seam, buttons and buttonholes patterned, or a stitched border emphasising the fastening, neck and sleeves.

To give a personal touch to her home by her own thought and handiwork comes naturally to an Englishwoman. Here embroidery can play its part, for having so many ways and means it can adapt itself appropriately to the many subjects that the house presents. Let us beware lest the curtain or cloth be the worse for its added ornament ! Household linen does not call for decoration of an ambitious order, nor need such objects have a great amount of work upon them, for this would be misplaced energy which should be reserved for bigger undertakings. A neat and somewhat monotonous pattern, worked perhaps in white, is appropriate for table linen. The design may be of a geometrical or strictly formal floral type, or simply lines of pretty stitching. Such patterns are not too noticeable, which is a point in their favour, for we do not want constantly to be struck by marvellous decoration upon objects in daily use. All that is required is a pleasant consciousness that something not absolutely necessary has been added, making the object individual as well as useful. For such subjects as seat covers and cushions, there is canvas work, used and known in the Middle Ages as *opus pulvinarium*, or cushion style. Its technique is durable and its patterns are decorative. For such objects as hangings, screens and quilts, the Jacobean work was a fine creation, but nowadays it has been cheapened by weak imitation. For a change, designs for large surfaces such as hangings or quilts, based on geometrical elements, knot-work or counterchanges, look well. An example of a hanging, and of a screen, decorated with knot-work ornament, is shown in Plates II, IIA, XVIA and XVIIA. Needlework is pleasing for wall decoration, either framed or filling panels. Further discussion on the uses and designs for embroidery are unnecessary, for the wise worker who has begun to take interest in stitches and design will have alert eyes to see the many opportunities that lie before her for the cunning display of her art. She will do well to note how in times past her ancestors left traces of the needle's art upon all the fabrics that they touched. Aided by the knowledge with which her searchings into the past will supply her, she will endeavour to do her part and hand on to another generation our glorious and dignified tradition of the fine art of needlework.

CHAPTER II—FLAT STITCHES

AS stitches will now be the main subject of discussion, a preliminary classification will be an orderly way of entering upon it. A single flat stitch, best illustrated by Stem, is the foundation from which all others develop. Stitches may be divided into four main groups. These are Flat, Looped, Chained, and Knotted. The most widely practised of the first group is Satin, which is composed of a number of flat stitches laid side by side in close parallel lines. Other typical ones are Couching, Darning, and Laid Work. The first deviation from a straight stitch is a looped one. For this the flat stitch is pulled out of the straight and forced into a loop by another passing across it. Buttonhole may be taken as the typical example of this second group. Others are Feather, Scroll, and Diamond. A complete loop becomes a chain, and the many varieties of Chain compose the third group. A chain twisted up tightly develops into a knot, and the knots, exemplified by Bullion, French, and Trellis, fill the fourth and last main group. Other less fundamental divisions are easily formed—for instance, the Canvas stitches. These are gathered from the first three main groups, and applied to a particular kind of ground fabric, which gives them their distinctive character and name. The Composite stitches are of all kinds, their chief feature being that they consist of one stitch imposed upon another, as for example Interlacing or Pekinese. Cut Work is another distinct kind and the Drawn Fabric stitches form a group to themselves.

STEM STITCH, figure 1.—The diagram explains the working of this stitch, known also as Crewel or Outline. During the working, the thread must be kept to the same side of the needle, either to the left or to the right, as suits the purpose in hand. In the diagram, a fairly broad stem line is in process of working. If a finer line is required, the needle must both enter and return through the material exactly upon the traced line. To raise a stem line, run a thread along the tracing and work the stitches over it. The piece of material picked up by the needle for each stitch may vary in size. It is perhaps most usual to pick up only as much as is necessary to hold ; another method is to work so that a regular line of Back stitching is formed upon the under side. This is contrived by picking up a piece of material exactly upon the traced line, just half the length of the stitch. Stem makes a satisfactory filling stitch. When used for this purpose the lines of the filling usually follow round the outline and further interest may be given by adding gradation of colour. Figure 2 shows a Stem-stitch filling worked in a special manner. By working thus a neat pattern of diagonal bands is formed over the surface which would under usual treatment have been plain. Patterning a flat surface has a refining effect, also it suggests an all-pervading orderliness which is a pleasing quality in design. When this new form of Stem-stitch filling follows a curve, instead of a straight line as in the diagram, the effect is better. The worker should experiment with it upon such objects as tree trunks, birds, or animals. (See Plates XII and XIII.) In such cases the lines of stitching usually follow round with the outline of the form to be filled. The execution is as follows: Begin at the lower left-hand corner of figure 2, and work a single, upright line of neat Stem stitching. Make all the stitches of exactly the same length, and insert the needle perpendicularly,

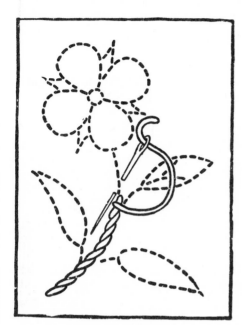

FIG. I. STEM STITCH.

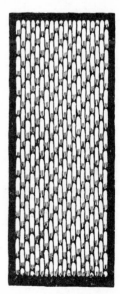

FIG. 2. STEM-STITCH FILLING.

let it pick up a piece of material just one-third the length of the stitch, and let the working thread lie upon the right of the needle. At the end of a line, fasten off the thread and begin again at the base. Keep each succeeding line of stitching close to the previous one, and with each new row insert the needle a step above the point where it entered for the row before. It is this regular step up which gives the pretty diagonal stripes to the solid mass of stitching. LINE SHADING, figure 3.—This is another way to work Stem stitch fillings. The method is as much used for contrast as for gradual change in tone, and by its means all kinds of pretty effects can be obtained. This type of work has been carried to perfection in the Dutch East Indian embroideries of early eighteenth-century date. In fact, in most Eastern Chain stitch work, this method of filling up the forms by contrasted lines of different colours is adopted. Fillings formed thus add great refinement and interest to the detail of the design; there are few prettier methods employed for the execution of fine embroidery than this. (See figures 52A and 52B.)

WHIPPED STEM STITCH, figure 4.—When executing bold lines in Stem, it is sometimes a good plan to whip over the finished line of stitching. When the row is completed, the needle works the thread gradually back to the starting-point, passing it, at regular intervals, round the line of Stem stitching.

SATIN STITCH, figure 5.—In the diagram, Satin is being used upon an ivy leaf, which has been divided up into panels so that the stitches should not be unnecessarily long, for when this is the case, Satin is inclined to look loose and untidy, and to wear badly. For another reason it is often a good plan to break up a surface to be worked in flat Satin, as the change of direction of the threads causes a pretty play of light upon the colour. The stitches stretch from side to side of the space to be covered, and they are usually laid obliquely. A technical difficulty with Satin is the attainment of a neat firm line at both sides of a filling.

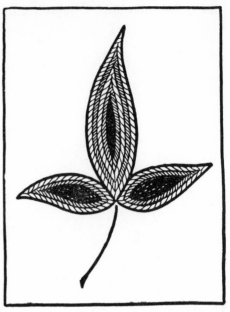

FIG. 3. LINE SHADING IN STEM STITCH

This is well mastered in Chinese embroidery, where the well-drawn edge is especially insisted upon. Often a narrow margin of fabric is left visible between the many petals of a large double flower carried out in Satin. This is called 'voiding,' and serves to emphasise the shape.

SATIN WORKED BY THE COUNTED THREADS OF THE GROUND FABRIC, figure 6.—On the early English samplers, geometrical patterns executed in Satin are commonly seen, and they are often combined with Cut Work, for the two kinds of embroidery go well together.

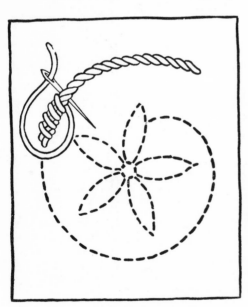

FIG. 4. WHIPPED STEM STITCH.

This is a pretty treatment of Satin, for it gives a formalism to the design which is always satisfactory in decorative work. Even-meshed hand-woven linen makes the best material for the ground, and the thread should match it in both tone and texture. Both should be

PLATE IV. LIGHT FILLINGS FOR LEAVES. *Outlines of leaves, scrolling stem and margin, in Pekinese stitch.*

PLATE V. THE PARK. *Worked throughout in Buttonhole stitch.*

of good quality, for the intrinsic worth of fine linen is a valuable asset to an embroidery. There is little to learn in the technique. The stitching must be exact to a thread, or the forms will lose their sharp outlines. The thread must be just the size to fill the required space. The chief stitch used in this type of work is Satin, besides which, Overcast and Buttonhole wheels are frequently added, for they make a contrast to the other part ; also Holbein stitch is used for any line work. Figures 6 and 9A, also Plate III, each contain a collection of useful patterns for the work. Any of the elements illustrated can be used independently if need be.

SATIN STITCH SHADING, figure 7.—With Satin, shading is usually effected in definite bands; if more gradual change of tone were required, Long and Short or Crewel stitch would be employed instead. There are three chief methods of shading in Satin. The first, that in which the successive bands of varying tone just touch each other at the edges ; a second, where the bands slightly encroach upon each other ; and a third, when the bands are, what is termed, voided. Of the three, the Chinese method of voiding is the most difficult, for the narrow lines of exposed fabric, although built up by many stitches, have to appear as firmly drawn as a pen-and-ink line. To execute Satin in encroaching fashion, as in figure 7, each new stitch is made to fit in between two of the row before. The encroachment is usually a bare sixteenth of an inch.

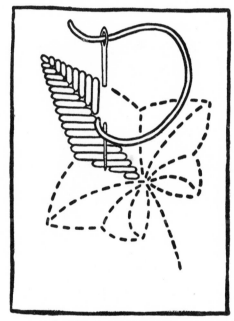

FIG. 5. SATIN STITCH.

LONG AND SHORT STITCH, figure 8.—This is a variation of Satin. Instead of working the stitches all of one length, they are worked alternately long and short, and are so arranged that on one side of the band of stitching a firm edge is kept, and on the other a dentated line. The leaf in figure 8 shows a band of Long and Short upon the margin in a dark shade, the remainder of the leaf being filled in with another form of Satin. The advantage of commencing with a line of Long and Short stitch for a solid filling is that an irregular line is formed on the inner edge, into which another shade of colour can be easily blended. Again, if Long and Short stitch is used for an edging in outline work, the inner edge thus broken is softer and more pleasing. The method of work is the same as for Satin. For Long and Short stitch to be properly effective there must be a distinct difference in the length of the stitches. This long and short treatment of a stitch can be applied to other

FIG. 6. A COLLECTION OF PATTERNS TAKEN FROM ENGLISH SAMPLERS.

varieties besides Satin. Buttonhole stitch lends itself admirably to being worked in this way, either for the edge of a leaf or a border line.

LONG AND SHORT STITCH (VARIATION), figure 9.—This is an economical method of working Long and Short stitch. With it there is little thread wasted on the under side of the fabric. Upon the surface the two are almost identical, but the method of execution is different. Unless special care is taken, there is a danger of this stitch being less firm in line upon the outer edge than the other. Upon the right-hand form in figure 9, the longer of the two stitches is seen in process of formation. For the second, shorter one, the needle, instead of coming through upon the margin as in the usual stitch, is brought through at the point

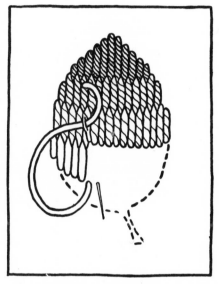

FIG. 7. SHADING BY MEANS OF BANDS OF ENCROACHING SATIN STITCH.

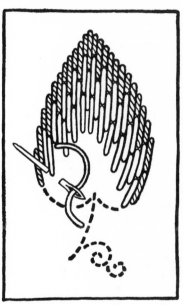

FIG. 8. LONG AND SHORT STITCH.

which marks the base of the shorter stitch. (See needle in diagram.) This stitch, worked but loosened, is seen in the left-hand form, also the small piece of material upon the margin, which is next picked up by the needle in order to be in correct position for working the next long stitch. This can also be seen worked though again left quite loose, and the end of the thread is in evidence emerging from the material at the correct point for working the next short stitch. The short traced line, seen in the diagram, connecting two threads, represents the only portion of working thread occurring upon the back of the fabric.

BRICK STITCH SHADING, figure 10.—This is the name given to a method of shading which is carried out with extreme regularity, the work being executed by Long and Short and Satin stitches. The stitches should all be parallel, without any suggestion of radiation. The first row is composed of Long and Short, and the remainder of the filling is of Satin stitches of equal length. The stitch is often found upon the English seventeenth-century wool work hangings, where so many examples of shading methods can be studied with advantage.

SHADING STITCHES.—Shading used in right ways adds charm to embroideries, but when used wrongly it develops bad types of work. It should not be employed to make forms stand out in semblance of reality, for an embroidery representation of a subject must not aim at being realistic or even pictorial. Shading should not be used for the purpose of giving the composition an appearance of being definitely lighted from one side or other of the subject, for this gives a somewhat theatrical effect of light and shade. It can, however, safely be used to add variety to colour and thus enhance its beauty, to vary tone, and to

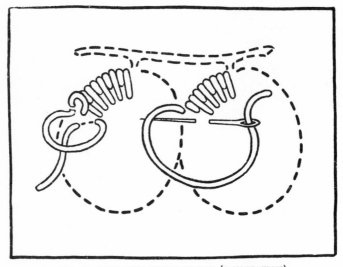

FIG. 9. LONG AND SHORT STITCH (A VARIATION).

provide a necessary contrast against a changing background and pattern. A point to be remembered, when shading is introduced, is that gradation of colour or tone requires as good drawing as an outline. The passage from one tone to another is usually better when definitely marked, rather than when blended imperceptibly, and it is necessary that the lines formed by this definite change of tone should be firmly drawn and of correct shape.

FLAT STITCH, figure 11.—A simple and useful variety for working solid fillings. For small leaves and petals of flowers it can be used as illustrated in the diagram. For larger forms, bands of the stitching must be worked side by side until the required space is filled in. The successive bands of a Flat stitch filling should be so joined that they interlock slightly with each other, for then the junction of the bands, instead of looking rather poor and thin, appears practically the same as the middle portion of the stitch. This is one of the smooth, even stitches which show fine floss silk to great advantage. The execution is explained by the diagram. The process there seen occurs alternately on either side

FIG. 9A. COLLECTION OF PATTERNS FROM A SPANISH SAMPLER, SIGNED DONNA MARIA DE LA BLANCO, DATED 1772.

of the leaf until the filling is completed. The special character of the stitch lies in the undulation of the surface which is made by the thread as it passes to and fro across the form.

FISHBONE STITCH, figure 12.—Though well adapted for working leaves this stitch can also be used for border lines and it can be executed either in one colour or in a contrasted chequering of two. When carried out in chequered colours the effect much resembles that of a wood-inlay pattern, and the embroidered chequering gives the same attractive appearance to a piece of embroidery that the inlay does to a panel of furniture. Shading in this stitch, or any requisite change of colour, is easily manipulated by bringing through at the required point another needle threaded with the fresh colour. The two needlefuls can be kept going and be brought alternately into

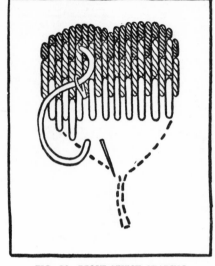

FIG. 10. BRICK STITCH SHADING.

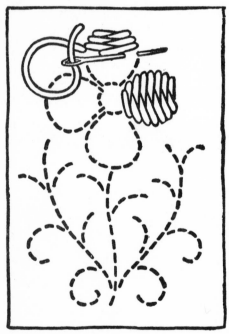

FIG. 11. FLAT STITCH.

use. To work Fishbone, bring the needle through at the apex of the leaf, and take a short straight stitch in the direction of the central vein. Then bring the needle to the surface, on the margin of the leaf, on the right side of and near the point where it first came through. Next take it to the back a little below the base of the first stitch and just across the central vein line. This second stitch should slant a little and each succeeding one slant a little more until the correct angle is obtained. For the third stitch, bring the needle out upon the opposite margin, again close to the first stitch, but this time on the left side. Take it through to the back as before on the far side of the central vein. If the stitches which meet at the centre were inserted exactly on the central vein, the material would incline to show through at this point, but crossing them well over each time prevents this.

RAISED FISHBONE STITCH, figure 13.—To carry out this stitch, bring the thread through at the apex of the leaf. Return it to the back upon the centre vein at a point nearly half-way down its length. Next bring the needle through on the left margin of the leaf, opposite the point in the centre where it has just gone through. An arrow on the diagram points to the correct spot for this. Next insert the needle on the right margin of the leaf, near the apex, and bring it to the front again on the left margin exactly opposite. Next insert the needle lower down on the leaf on the right margin, then pass it horizontally under the leaf and bring it to the surface on the opposite margin. The process so far described can be seen worked on the lowest leaf in the diagram. Next insert the needle again on the right margin close under the second stitch, and then bring it to the surface exactly opposite on the left margin. This process of passing the needle and thread horizontally underneath the

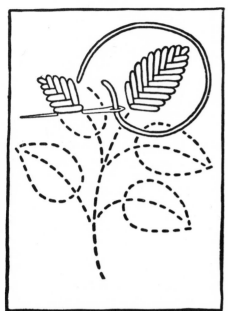

FIG. 12. FISHBONE STITCH.

leaf from margin to margin, alternately near the apex and then lower down, and thus building up two lines of slanting and crossing stitches, is continued until the leaf is completely covered up. It should then have the appearance of the top leaf of the spray.

OPEN FISHBONE STITCH, figure 14.—To work this, bring the needle through on the left side of and close to the vein, not far below the apex, and insert it at point A on the diagram. Next bring it through on the left margin opposite. Now pass the thread to the back upon the right side of the vein, a little below the

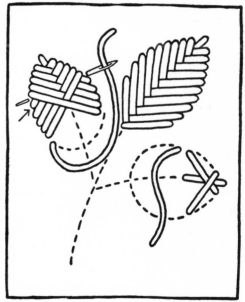

FIG. 13. RAISED FISHBONE STITCH.

starting point, and bring it to the surface upon the left side of the vein, opposite the point where it just entered. The thread is now in position to commence the third stitch, which is a repetition of the first.

c

LEAF STITCH, figure 15.—This diagram shows a light filling for a leaf or border line. To work the stitch bring the thread through at the base of the leaf to the left of the centre. Then insert the needle on the oppo-

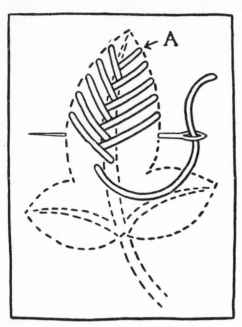

site margin, part way up the leaf, and bring it through to the surface again at the base, a little to the right of the centre and below the stitch, which now lies across the leaf. Next insert the needle upon the left-hand margin and bring it through again below in the same manner as previously, but upon the left side of the centre. Continue working alternately upon either side until the surface is lightly covered over. To complete the leaf, work some firm kind of stitch round the edge.

BASKET STITCH, figure 16.— In the diagram this stitch is worked closely; it can, however, be more open than this and allow the ground to show between the

FIG. 14. OPEN FISHBONE STITCH.

interlacing threads. To begin working, bring the thread through at the top of the left traced line. Insert it on the other traced line a little lower down, and then bring it through again on the line immediately opposite. Again insert the needle on the opposite side but above the stitch already there, and bring it through on the other line, just below where the thread first came through. Insert the needle again on the other side, underneath the stitch already there, and bring it out just opposite. It will be seen that to work Basket stitch the needle takes a step forward and backward alternately, and the reverse side

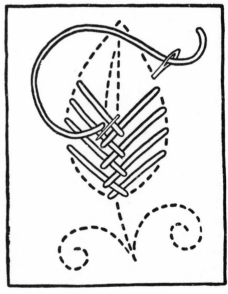

FIG. 15. LEAF STITCH.

should exhibit a series of parallel transverse threads occurring regularly two together, and then an interval between. The needle at work in the diagram shows the stage when the backward stitch is taken. Basket needs working regularly to look well, and the backward stitch must be taken into the actual perforations made by two previous stitches.

DOUBLE BACK STITCH, figure 17.—The diagram explains the method of work. First on one side and then on the other, the needle picks up a small portion of material. This process carries the thread to and fro from side to side, which results in a pretty plait-like effect upon the form it covers. If correctly worked the stitches should build up a double row of Back stitches upon the reverse side of the material. When working upon transparent stuff, such as batiste or muslin, a neat adaptation of this stitch can be contrived by making what is usually the reverse, the right or upper side. The Back stitches then make the out-

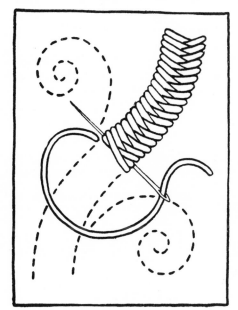

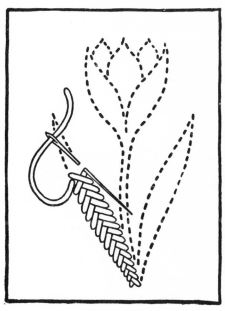

FIG. 16. BASKET STITCH.

FIG. 17. DOUBLE BACK STITCH.

line of the form and the crossing to and fro underneath peeps prettily through. It is as easy to work in the reverse as in the ordinary way. Double Back is a pleasant alternative to the more common Satin, and it is easier, quicker, and more economical in thread. Frequently it is employed for the execution of an entire piece of work, for it is equally good for lines or forms varying in width. When used as a filling for leaves or petals, an outline stitch may be added, but as a rule this is not an improvement. There are slight variations possible in the working. In the diagram the crossing threads lie close together ; it is possible, however, by picking up the ground material at less close intervals, to work more openly and let the ground show through between the crossing threads.

ROUMANIAN STITCH, figure 18.—This makes an excellent filling for a broad stem or border line. There are many slightly different ways of working it, the necessary characteristic being one long stitch tied down by a shorter one taken across it. Sometimes the tying down part of the stitch looks best taken straight across at right angles, but in figure 18, the form which has an oblique transverse stitch is illustrated. A slight variation would be to make the crossing stitch pull the longer part down, so that it takes a V-shape instead of going straight across. To work Roumanian stitch, bring the thread through at the top left-hand side of the space to be covered. Take it to the back upon the opposite margin of the petal and bring the needle through again just a little before the centre, and above the half worked stitch. Take it to the back, below the stitch now laid upon the surface (see dot in diagram). For the next stitch, bring the thread through to the surface upon the left-hand margin, immediately below the point where it first emerged. If the thread is thick and the stitches have to be very close together, it is often a good plan to bring up the thread for the transverse stitch through the centre of the crossing stitch above. This results in

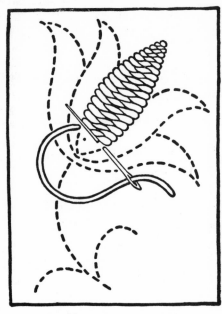

FIG. 18. ROUMANIAN STITCH.

a neatly chained line down the centre instead of a rather clumsy ill-fitting one.

CHEVRON STITCH, figure 19.—The diagram represents a neat little stitch founded on the plain needlework Herringbone. It is mainly used for border lines and is quick and easy to execute. In the lower portion of the figure, a block of the stitching has been drawn out in order to show how it may also be turned to good use as an all-over stitch for a light filling. (See Plate XII.) A pretty addition is to twist a thread of contrasting colour in and out of the line of stitching. The effect of this can be seen in Plate IX, where both ways of working are illustrated, and it is done in exactly the same way as that shown in figure 99. To work Chevron stitch, bring the thread through on the lower of the two traced lines at the left end. Then insert the needle about an eighth of an inch to the right of the commencement, and bring it through

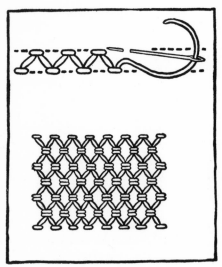

FIG. 19. CHEVRON STITCH.

to the surface, on the traced line, at a point exactly in the centre of the stitch now in process of formation. Next insert the needle upon the upper traced line farther along to the right, and bring it through to the surface a little to the left of the point where it has just entered (see needle in diagram). Next take the needle to the back a little farther along the line towards the right and bring it to the front again at the centre of the stitch now in process of being formed. If worked correctly the needle should have come up at the point just where it first entered the upper traced line. To continue, take the stitches alternately upon the upper and lower lines in the manner described.

ARROW-HEAD STITCH, figure 20.—This may be used either as a line stitch or as a light filling, as shown in the diagram, either for de-

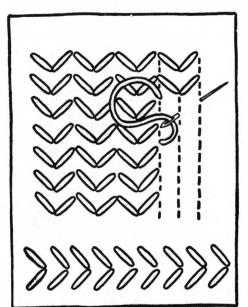

FIG. 20. ARROW-HEAD STITCH.

tails of the pattern or for the background. Again, it may be used as a powdered pattern with each pair of stitches detached from the rest. To work Arrow-Head stitch, bring the thread through at the top of the traced line most to the left. Insert the needle on the centre line and bring it up on the right-hand one, just as shown by the needle in the diagram. Next insert the needle on the central line at the point where it last entered. This completes the first stitch, and to continue bring the needle through at the correct place on the left-hand line for forming the next. The two stitches should slant at a right

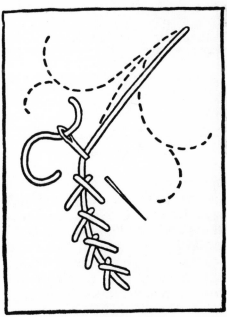

FIG. 21. THORN STITCH.

angle towards each other and they should be equally spaced apart. THORN STITCH, figure 21.—A useful variety for representing feather or fern lines or thorned stems, for the continuous unbroken line which occurs down the centre has a good effect. To work the spray illustrated in the diagram, bring the thread through at the apex of the traced line and take it to the back at the base. Leave this long thread, now lying upon the surface, slack enough to lie easily along the curve. Bring the needle to the front again a little to the left of the point where it last went through. Next insert the needle just over the central traced line, keeping the laid thread to the left of it, and bring it to the surface on the same side of the central line opposite the point where it last came through (see needle in diagram). Now pass the needle to the back at a point on the left side of the laid thread, opposite the stitch previously worked. This completes the first pair of stitches.

FERN STITCH, figure 22.—A simple variety useful for working feathery

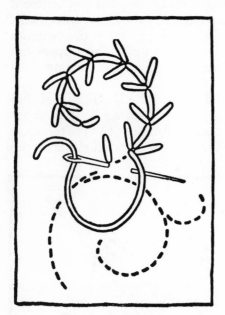

FIG. 22. FERN STITCH.

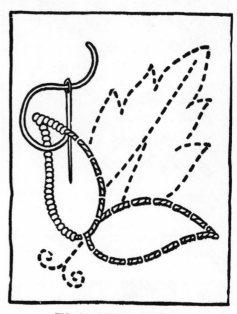

FIG. 23. OVERCAST STITCH.

sprays, open border lines, light veinings for leaves, or scrolling background patterns. It is composed of three single stitches of about the same length, which radiate from a common centre. The diagram explains the working. The three single stitches of which it is composed are worked in succession, and then the next group is commenced. The stitches, though usually of a like size, may vary in length. For instance, the lateral stitches may be required to be close together, in this case the centre stitch must be proportionately shorter.

OVERCAST STITCH, figure 23.—This well-known stitch is indispensable for that dainty branch of the art of needlework, fine white embroidery. It is used for working stems, outlining leaves and other forms which are afterwards to be filled in with a variety of fancy stitchings. In many kinds of coloured embroidery Overcast is also useful. For example, in fine heraldic work there is no better stitch than this for outlining either the shields or the forms figured upon them, also in cut and applied work, for a firm and secure edge is made by it. For perfect technique the help of a frame is required. To execute it, first run, or couch down, a thread of the requisite coarseness upon the traced line, and then cover it closely over with regular stitches in the manner illustrated in the diagram, always taking care to pick up as little as possible of the material underneath the laid thread, otherwise the raised line will not have the full round appearance which should characterise it. Another way to work Overcast is explained on page 73.

WHIPPED SATIN STITCH, figure 24.—A light Overcasting stitch is frequently added as a finish to other varieties. In the diagram it is placed over Satin. In the same manner Chain, Coral or Back stitch can sometimes be overcast with good effect.

DOT STITCH, figure 25.—This consists of a couple of Back stit-

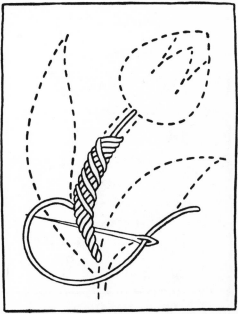

FIG. 24. WHIPPED SATIN STITCH.

ches worked one after the other into the same hole, and then a short interval is allowed before working a second couple. In the diagram, the stitch is used to vein a leaf. Sometimes these dots are spaced regularly over the surface of a petal as a powdering. They are not so effective if treated as run stitches, for the Back stitch formation makes them stand up better. A flowing line effect instead of a staccato one can be obtained by threading another strand in and out of the dots, as shown in the lower part of the figure.

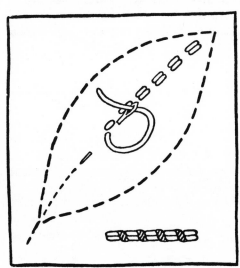

FIG. 25. DOT STITCH.

BACK STITCH, figure 26.—To show to most advantage, Back stitch should be worked with fairly coarse untwisted thread. The effect of a completed line of it should resemble a neat row of pearls, and this effect cannot be attained if too thin a thread or too long a stitch is employed. The worked line, though built up of many minute stitches, should have the appearance of being well and firmly drawn. The needle brings the thread through from the back about one-sixteenth of an inch or less from the beginning of the line to be worked. It then returns to the back at the commencement and comes through again a step beyond the starting-point, as can be seen in the diagram. This stitch is often used as a foundation for others. A pretty cord-like effect is obtained by threading in and out, through each stitch in succession, a silk of a contrasting colour. This method of working is shown in the lower portion of the diagram. A fine thread should be used for the added stitch or the under one will be too much covered. A minute piece of the ground material may, if necessary, be picked up as the needle passes under each Back stitch, if this makes the line more firmly drawn. Variations of a similar kind can be made by devising new methods of threading in and out. Some of these are illustrated in figures 102, 103, and 123

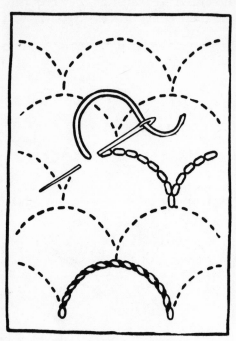

FIG. 26. BACK STITCH.

CHAPTER III—LOOPED STITCHES

THE looped stitches, a most useful group, are mainly varieties of Buttonhole. In mediæval embroidery there is no evidence of their use. This was probably because the work was then all done in the frame, and these are, by their nature, hand stitches. In the famous Elizabethan dress embroidery, of which figure 28 is an example, Buttonhole was much used for leaf fillings, and surely no prettier method of working these could have been devised. Figure 27, an enlarged detail of a portion of the tunic, gives some idea of how these were executed. Lines of stitching are taken to and fro across the leaf and effective use is made of both colour and shading. In the sixteenth century all arts reflected the prevailing spirit of romance. The designs for embroidery were full of imagination, variety, and pretty surprises. Look at the fantastic mixture of flowers, birds, butterflies and other insects displayed upon this coat! Add to the attractiveness of the design its execution in various brightly coloured silks, leaves shading quite happily from blue through green to salmon-pink, a golden plaited stem curving in and out binding all together—we have in this example of English embroidery a beautiful and characteristic piece belonging to that interesting period.

FIG. 27. DETAIL FROM FIG. 28.

BUTTONHOLE STITCH, figure 29.—Buttonhole makes an excellent edging stitch and is frequently put to this use, either for making secure the

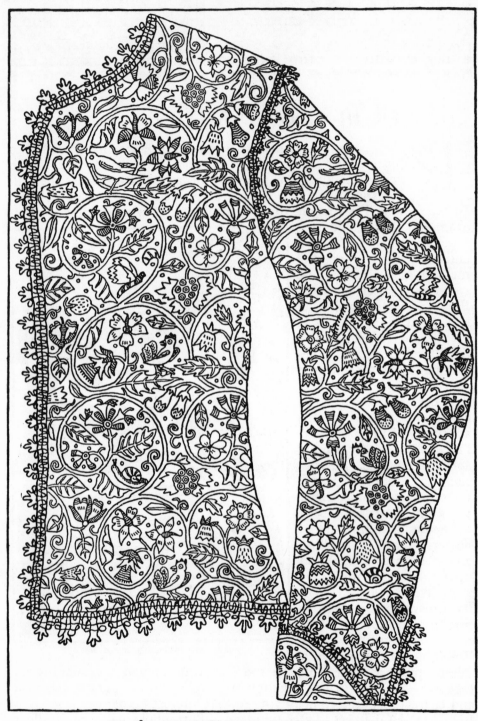

FIG. 28. A SIXTEENTH-CENTURY EMBROIDERED JACKET.

cut material in open work, or for binding other raw edges. Used as a filling or for lines Buttonhole can be employed in a number of different ways. When employed for fillings each succeeding row of stitching is worked into the heading of the previous row, no matter whether the stitch is being treated in open or close fashion. The lines of buttonholing are sometimes taken straight across the surface to be covered, at other times they follow round the outline. Frequently for solid fillings, a line of thread is thrown across from side to side and the stitch worked over this as well as into the heading of the row before. This suggests another use for buttonholing, which is to couch down various forms of laid threads. The couched thread may be a gold or silver one and this with fine floss silk buttonholing it down is most delicate and pretty. An open flower can have the metal thread couched spirally from near the centre to the outside, where some solid Satin or Buttonhole stitching in silk finishes it off. Equally satisfactory is the method of letting the couching thread start round the outline and

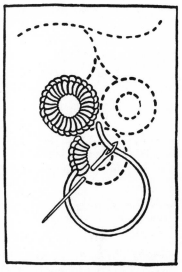

FIG. 29. BUTTONHOLE STITCH.

continue round and round until the form is completely filled in. There are still other uses to which this stitch may be applied. For instance, backgrounds needing light decoration can be covered with open buttonholing which gives the effect of an all-over honeycomb patterning. A variation of the ordinary buttonhole edging is to roll the raw edge over a fine cord and buttonhole over this in some fanciful way, such as three close stitches followed by an interval, and so on. How to work Buttonhole is explained by the diagram, figure 29, where it is forming a thick outline to some berries. Here the stitch is worked in close fashion, the open form only differing in having each stitch slightly separated from the one on either side. Buttonhole wheels, a

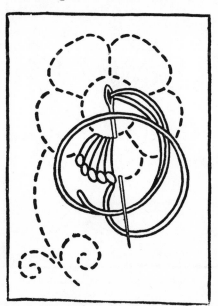

FIG. 30. TAILOR'S BUTTONHOLE STITCH.

useful form of this stitch, are worked like the berries in the diagram, only the needle passes into the exact same hole in the centre each time. Plate V illustrates the usefulness and adaptability of this stitch ; it is entirely executed by its means.

TAILOR'S BUTTONHOLE, figure 30.—This variation on the ordinary Buttonhole is useful in both plain and fancy needlework. The difference between it and the usual form is that there is an additional knot at the heading, which gives it a firmer and more ornamental appearance. Tailor's Buttonhole cannot be satisfactorily worked when the stitches are spaced far apart, because the heading knot needs support on either side to keep it rigid. A possible variation lies in the change of length of the straight portion of the stitch, for this part, by varying in some regular sequence, can be made to form vandykes or chequers such as those shown in figure 31. Worked in this way it makes a decorative border line. The stitch is perhaps most used for working small petals or leaves. Figure 30 explains the execution. For the first part of the working, treat it exactly like the simpler variety—that is, work as directed for figure 29. When in the position illustrated by that diagram, proceed to take hold of the thread where it is doubled, fairly near the eye of the needle, and pass it under the point from right to left, so that it takes the position illustrated in figure 30. Then pull the needle through over the threads which now lie under it, and the stitch is complete.

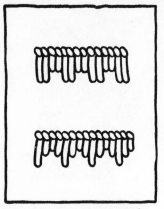

FIG. 31. BANDS IN TAILOR'S BUTTONHOLE.

KNOTTED BUTTONHOLE STITCH, figure 32.—This is the ordinary variety with the addition of a knot at the apex. For such a purpose as that illustrated in the diagram, the added knot is an improvement. Worked in coarse thread, as an edging to a design, the stitch suggests a knotted fringe. To work knotted Buttonhole bring the thread through at the left-hand end of the traced line. Pass the working thread once round the thumb of the left hand which will now be holding the material near to the starting-point, and then transfer the loop

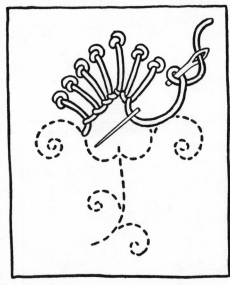

FIG. 32. KNOTTED BUTTONHOLE STITCH.

thus formed on to the needle by passing this up through the loop in the manner illustrated in figure 33. Then with the loop round the needle, continue to work the Buttonhole stitch in the usual way. When the stage figured in the working diagram is reached the thread should be lightly pulled so that both the knot and the buttonhole loop, which are in process of formation, are fairly tight before the needle is finally pulled through. This method of forming a knot by first twisting the thread round the thumb should be noted, for some find it an easy method of making other embroidery knots.

DETACHED BUTTONHOLE STITCH, figure 34.—One method of using Buttonhole stitch for flower petals is to work it almost entirely detached from the ground fabric. The diagram shows such a petal in process of execution. Towards the right-hand end of the line the stitches are shown separated, this is only to explain the execution. They should lie close together as on the left side. To commence working the petal a foundation composed of two long Satin stitches is laid upon the material, stretching from corner to corner of the outer edge. The first row of stitching is worked over this two-

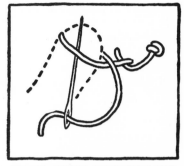

FIG. 33. DETAIL OF WORKING THE KNOT.

fold line of thread, and the succeeding rows are worked into the heading of the row before. For stability the first and last stitches of the first row are stitched into the ground fabric as well as over the laid threads. To execute a petal, the buttonholing must be worked continuously to and fro, first from right to left, and then left to right. After the first three rows, the number of stitches is gradually decreased until at the base of the petal only three stitches compose the last row. At this point, a single stitch, taken from the last row into the ground fabric, fixes the base of the petal to the material. The petal should not lie flatly upon the ground, it should have a convex shape like those in the sampler, Plate VI.

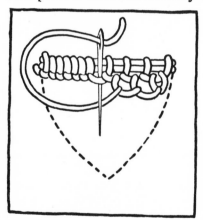

FIG. 34. DETACHED BUTTONHOLE STITCH.

Say a petal commences with fifteen stitches in the uppermost row, then each fresh petal must commence with the same number, or they will not be of like size when finished. The necessary decrease in the number of stitches in each line must only take place at the end of a row. The chief technical difficulty with this method of work is to keep the stitch neat and firm at the extremities of a line at the point where the turn has to be made to come back. These successive turning stitches eventually form the side margins of the petal, and if, in the working, a loose and irregular line is built up, the result is most unsatisfactory. One aid to this is to keep the thread tight at the turn of each line of stitching. For the technique to be perfect, much depends upon the employment of the right type of thread. That, in the sampler, is a firm, fairly coarse linen of even texture. This type of work is usually done with white linen thread on a ground of white or stone-coloured linen, but it can look well in colour. The flowers and leaves in Plate VI are all executed in Detached Buttonhole, also those in the centre of Plate XVII.

BUTTONHOLE STITCH SHADING, figure 35.—This is a useful shading stitch, and there are a number of ways in which it can be adapted to this purpose. When Buttonhole is employed as a solid filling, it is usual to work each fresh row over the heading of the previous row as illustrated in the diagram. The shading is contrived by working each row, or couple of rows, in a different colour or tone. The stitches can be close together or spaced slightly apart to show an under thread like that seen in the unfinished portion in the diagram. This underlay, which is usually added, can be of the same colour as the surface buttonholing, or

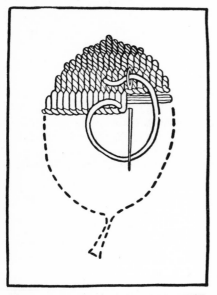

FIG. 35. SHADING IN BUTTONHOLE STITCH.

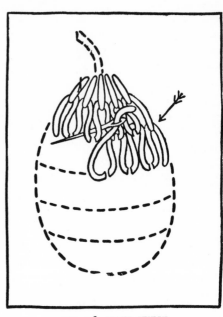

FIG. 36. WAVE STITCH.

it may be opposed to it. The former is the most simply worked, for at the end of a line the working thread is carried across from right to left and it is then in position for executing the next row of stitching. Sometimes all the shading is expressed by the underlay, and an openly spaced buttonholing, in a single tint, laid over it. An alternative method is to lay a pale bright colour underneath and vary the surface stitching. Forms can be shaded by this stitch in bands worked directly across or in bands following round the outline. The latter are well illustrated in Plate V. A pretty ribbed effect is obtained by working the narrowest possible band of close buttonholing over both the heading of the last row and a laid thread.

WAVE STITCH, figure 36.—In the diagram the effect of this stitch has been sacrificed to clearness of workmanship. In actual work, the loops are packed closely side by side, and do not show any ground fabric between. This stitch, most effective in woollen thread, is good for shading purposes, partly because of the manner in which the successive bands encroach upon each other. To carry out Wave stitch, commence at the apex with a band of radiating Satin stitches. Then bring the thread through upon the right-hand side of the form, at the base of what will be the second band of stitching (see arrow); next, pass the thread through the Satin stitch immediately above, in the manner shown by the needle lower down in the diagram. During the process, the needle does not enter the ground fabric. Next, pick up with the needle a very small piece of material, close to the starting-point of the present band and upon the traced line marking its base. Then proceed to pass the needle and thread as before through the second of the row of Satin stitches above. Continue the alternate action of first picking up material at the base of the band, then threading through the stitch above, until the end of the row is reached. Then commence the third band, again starting from the right side. The difference be-

tween the first and the later rows of stitching is that the thread may have to be, at the beginning, passed through single stitches instead of loops. The first row, however, can be looped like the others if there is sufficient space, but with a narrow apex, like that in the diagram, Satin generally fits in best. The individual stitches must be placed closely together, and not pulled at too great tension. The colours or tone of thread can vary with each row or even change in the same band if required.

LADDER STITCH, figure 37.—Though most frequently employed for the working out of straight or curved geometrical lines,

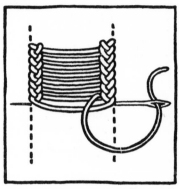

FIG. 37. LADDER STITCH.

Ladder can be used upon leaves or other forms of varying width. In the diagram, a broad line is being carried out. To begin working, bring the thread through at the upper end of the left-hand traced line. Return it to the back upon the other traced line exactly opposite and bring it through again close by, above the line just worked and on the inner side of the point where it last went through. Now take it to the back again upon the right-hand traced line just below the first stitch and bring it through to the surface upon the other traced line exactly opposite. The stage just described is illustrated by the needle. Next, the thread has to be looped through the completed stitch at each edge in turn. This is done first on the left-hand side by passing the needle, in the direction from above downwards, underneath the stitch close to the starting-point. The needle should be slanted outwards during the process. Next carry the thread across to the opposite side and there again loop it through the stitch above. This time the needle passes the thread horizontally underneath two crossed threads in the direction from right to left. This process has just been gone through by the last completed stitch illustrated in the diagram; in fact, by close examination of this last stitch the looping through for either edge can be followed out. The needle in the diagram shows how to continue.

CRETAN STITCH, figure 38.—This stitch, useful for broad lines or fillings, easily adapts itself to forms of varying width. If the space to be filled is of too large an area to be covered by a single band of the stitching, several rows of it can be placed side by side until the space is covered over. To work Cretan, as illustrated in the diagram, bring the needle through at the apex of the leaf. Take it to the back upon the right-hand margin, close to where it first came through and bring it to the front again at a point a little below this and rather nearer the centre of the leaf. The needle then pulls the thread through over the working thread and the same process is then repeated on the

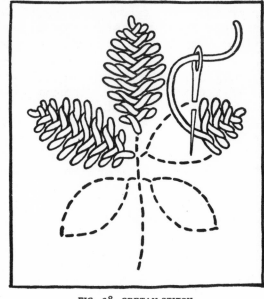

FIG. 38. CRETAN STITCH.

opposite side. For the remainder of the leaf, continue taking the stitches in similar fashion alternately on either side, always inserting the needle on the margin of the leaf. It would be just as easy to let the width of the central plait vary with the width of the leaf instead of the outer portion doing so. This result can be obtained by taking up with the needle, every time, an equal-sized piece of material. Whether variations in the shape occur or not, the proportionate width of the outer to the inner portion of Cretan stitch can always be regulated by the quantity of material picked up by the needle. Figure 39 illustrates Cretan worked in a slightly different form. The central plait pulls

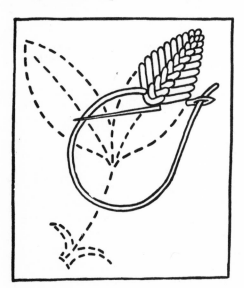

FIG. 39. CRETAN STITCH VARIATION.

the side portions down into a vandyke shape.

PLAITED EDGE STITCH, figure 40.—This is a useful stitch for covering a raw edge. In the diagram, two different ways of working it are shown, and the lower band of stitching exhibits the results given by both methods. The stitch can be used to cover a raw edge, selvedge, or hem ; for binding a raw edge of loosely woven fabric it is best to work by the first method. Begin by fixing the thread at the back at the point where the first needle in the figure is piercing the fabric. Then insert the needle as illustrated and pull through. A single upright stitch should now be lying on both upper and under surface. Next, pass the needle under this stitch in the manner shown by the second needle, not allowing it during the process to enter the ground fabric. The alternative method of working the second stage of the stitch is illustrated where the third needle is at work. Here, instead of passing under the stitch, the needle is passed a second time through the edge of the fabric.

FEATHER STITCH, figure 41.— Feather is worked in many different

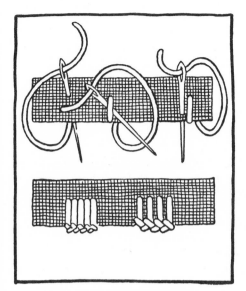

FIG. 40. PLAITED EDGE STITCH.

ways, all of which are based on the simple foundation illustrated in the diagram. The stitch is suitable for carrying out lines or fernlike leaves, and it would be an appropriate method for executing any kind of light all-over pattern upon a background. It makes also a pretty open filling for a large leaf if worked in lines suggestive of the veining. The diagram illustrates the working. The looped stitch seen in process of formation is worked alternately on either side. In figure 42 one of the simple variations of Feather stitch is illustrated. The working is similar to the former one, but the effect obtained is that of a zig-zagged line. CLOSED FEATHER STITCH, figure 43.—This makes a dainty

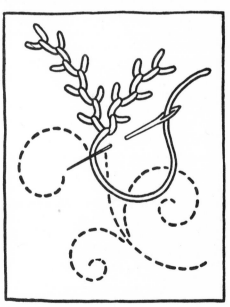

FIG. 41. FEATHER STITCH.

border and its effectiveness can sometimes be increased by inserting laid threads of a contrasting colour underneath, for this stitch can be used to couch down laid threads. Strands of bright-coloured silk are first laid or lightly darned on the material and the Feather stitch worked to and fro over them, preferably in some dark colour. To carry out the stitch as in figure 43, bring the thread through at the commencement of the left-hand traced line. Throw the working thread over to the right and insert the needle on the other traced line a little higher up than the starting-point, and bring it through a little below. Pull the needle through over the working thread. The needle in the diagram explains the second stitch, which is the same process in reverse direction on the other side. When picking up material with the needle, each time insert it close to the stitch above so that the thread joins on with no apparent break. Each fresh stitch should commence at a point just opposite the centre of the one last worked.

FIG. 42. DOUBLE FEATHER STITCH.

CHAINED FEATHER STITCH, figure 44.—A neat border stitch composed of a central zig-zag line with a Single Chain stitch attached at each recurring point. To work it bring the thread through at the top of the left-hand traced line and there work a Chain stitch in a slanting direction, just as the needle is doing a little lower down. Next insert the needle a little below to the right and bring it out on the right-hand traced line in correct position for working the second Chain stitch.

VANDYKE STITCH, figure 45.—Though often used as a border line, this variety can be adapted to the working of leaves and other fillings. The diagram explains the execution. Bring the needle through on the left traced line, then, in the centre between the two traced lines and about half an inch higher up, pick up a small portion of fabric. (See diagram.) Next, the needle passes the thread to the back upon the right-hand line, opposite the starting-point. For the second stitch, the thread is brought to the surface on the left line immediately below the first stitch. The second and all succeeding stitches are worked like the first excepting that the needle is at the centre slipped under the crossing of the stitch above, instead of into the fabric. If any difficulty is experienced in keeping the proper slant to the side stitches, the needle can enter the ground fabric each time it passes under the previous stitch.

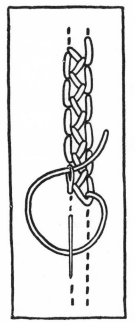

FIG. 43. CLOSED FEATHER STITCH.

LOOP STITCH, figure 46.—A useful light filling for a leaf or a broad line. To commence bring through the thread at the right-hand end of the band in the centre between the two traced lines. Insert the needle on the upper traced line a little to the left of the starting-point and bring it through again on the lower traced line immediately below The second stage of the working is illustrated by the needle at work. It should not, whilst looping through the thread, pierce the ground stuff underneath.

CEYLON STITCH, figure 47.—A useful close filling for a formal design. It also makes a decorative broad line. The stitch is worked by means of a series of chained loops which, by fastening one into the other, gradually build up a surface resembling a piece of plain knitting. The monotony of an extensive filling solidly worked in this stitch is relieved by making use of two contrasting colours arranged in bands across the surface, as in the lowest leaf in the worked example in Plate XVII. It is not necessary to place the chain loops as closely together as they are on this leaf. They can be spaced apart so as to show the connecting thread between. For many purposes it is more effective executed in this more open fashion, and it takes less time to do. To commence working, throw a strand of thread across the form. In the diagram the stitch has been commenced twice; a single stitch at the apex shows the start and the first loop, and lower down a series of the chained lines are shown, and where the needle is at work, the manner in which each fresh loop joins on to the one above it is illustrated. After throwing the preliminary line of thread across from left to right, the thread is passed under the material back again and comes up just below the starting-point. The thread is then looped into the laid line of thread as many times and as close together as may be necessary. It is easy to see what a practical stitch this would be for working in metal threads, for there is a minimum amount of passing to and fro through the material.

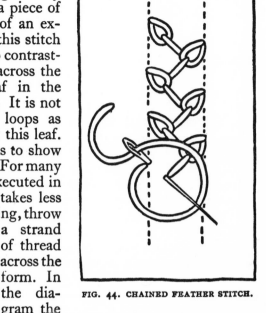

FIG. 44. CHAINED FEATHER STITCH.

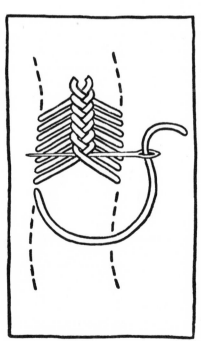

FIG. 45. VANDYKE STITCH.

DIAMOND STITCH, figure 48.—This attractive stitch makes a border or an insertion, and it could be used for an open filling for a leaf or for any larger form simply by increasing the number of stitches in a row to obtain the necessary width. In certain kinds of embroidery decorative stitchery is used to take the place of colour. On a window-blind, for example, colour would be useless, but patterned stitchery effective. The same would be true when working in white thread upon a dark material or the reverse. It is in such cases as these that the above stitch and other

like kinds would be employed to advantage. To execute Diamond stitch bring the thread through at the apex of the left-hand traced line. Insert it on the other line exactly opposite and bring it to the surface immediately below. Hold the working thread down upon the material, towards the left, with the thumb, and pass the needle under the two threads as shown in the diagram. When

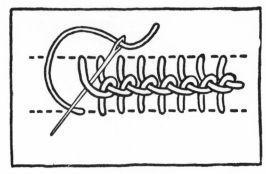

FIG. 46. LOOP STITCH.

the thread is pulled through, a knot will be seen upon the right side of the first stitch. Repeat the process on the left side of the same stitch so as to place a second knot upon it. When forming these first two knots, it is a good plan to pick up ground material at the same time. Next, pass the needle to the back immediately under the second knot and bring it to the surface one-sixteenth of an inch below. Now make a knot similar to the first two, but in the centre upon the lower of the two transverse stitches. Do not fix this one into the ground material. (See lower needle in diagram.) Next, the needle passes in and out of the ground fabric on the right-hand traced line, at the points marked by two dots in the figure. It is now in position to work the first knot again. Diamond stitch occurs in Plate XXXIV. This stitch can be worked over a padding of laid threads, thus turning it into a raised decorative band, or be thrown across an open space, this latter plan making an insertion of it. A variation is to work the stitch in a chequering of two colours as seen in Plate XIII. To work in two colours is easily contrived. When the first few knots are completed and the needle has

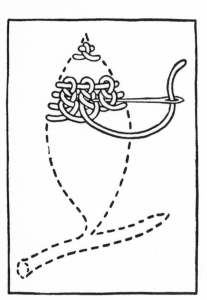

FIG. 47. CEYLON STITCH.

carried the thread to the back, then instead of bringing it to the surface again, bring a fresh thread through, and after that, a few stitches lower down, return by the same means to using the first one again.

SWORD-EDGING STITCH, figure 49.—This can be used as a crest-

PLATE VI. WILD ROSES. Leaves and Flowers in Detached Buttonhole stitch. Stems in Detached Overcast. Uprights in Composite stitches. Margin in Overcast Chain and Interlaced Band.

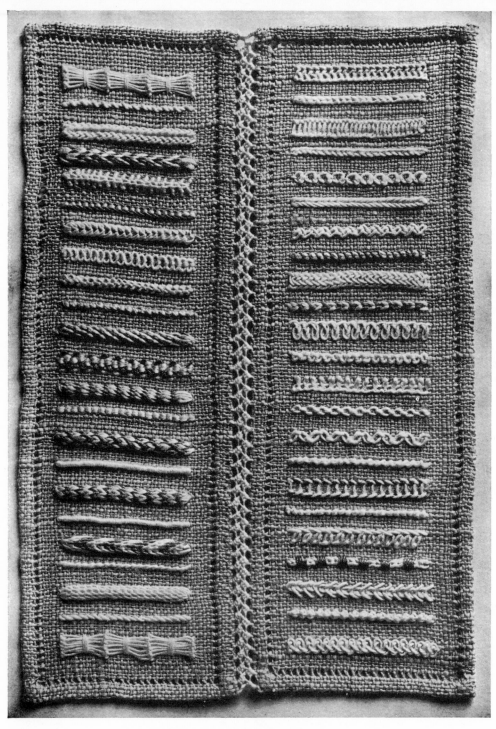

PLATE VII. Line Stitches (for names see next page).

First Row.	Second Row.
1. Sheaf.	1. Double Chain.
2. Whipped Run.	2. Chain.
3. Ceylon.	3. Open Chain.
4. Vandyked Chain Band.	4. Broad Chain.
5. Step.	5. Knotted Chain.
6. Pekinese.	6. Heavy Chain.
7. Portuguese Border.	7. Zigzag Chain.
8. Knotted Chain.	8. Whipped Chain.
9. Raised Chain Band.	9. Plaited Braid.
10. Whipped Back.	10. Chequered Chain.
11. Diagonal Woven Band.	11. Rosette Chain.
12. Threaded Back.	12. Knotted Chain.
13. Striped Woven Band.	13. Crested Chain.
14. Back Stitch.	14. Cable.
15. Chequered Chain Band.	15. Zigzag Cable.
16. Detached Overcast.	16. Twisted Chain.
17. Striped Chain Band.	17. Singalese Chain.
18. Overcast.	18. Coral.
19. Raised Chevron Stem.	19. Petal.
20. Stem.	20. Overcast Chain.
21. Raised Stem Band.	21. Wheat Ear.
22. Broad Stem.	22. Double Knot.
23. Sheaf.	23. Braid.

Italian Buttonhole Insertion.

First Row.	*Second Row.*

First Row.

1. Flat.
2. Split.
3. Crossed Buttonhole.
4. Double Buttonhole.
5. Threaded Chevron.
6. Threaded Back.
7. Raised Interlaced
   Herringbone.
8. Arrow Head.
9. Loop.
10. Couching.
11. Chained Feather.
12. Satin.
13. Closed Feather.
14. Long and Short.
15. Double Feather.
16. Spaced Buttonhole.
17. Tailor's Buttonhole.
18. Feather.
19. Knotted Buttonhole.
20. Rope.
21. Buttonhole.
22. Scroll.
23. Ladder.

Knotted Insertion combined with Braid Edging Stitch.

Second Row.

1. Raised Stem.
2. Interlacing.
3. Whipped Satin.
4. Guilloche.
5. Chevron.
6. Interlaced Band.
7. Fancy Couching.
8. Basket.
9. Bullion and French
   Knots.
10. Roumanian Vandyked
    and Chequered.
11. Diamond.
12. Roumanian.
13. Double Back.
14. Roumanian.
15. Laced Herringbone.
16. Open Cretan.
17. Twisted Lattice.
18. Cretan.
19. Tied Herringbone.
20. Vandyke.
21. Chained Border.
22. Chequered Fishbone.
23. Zigzag Coral.
24. Fishbone.

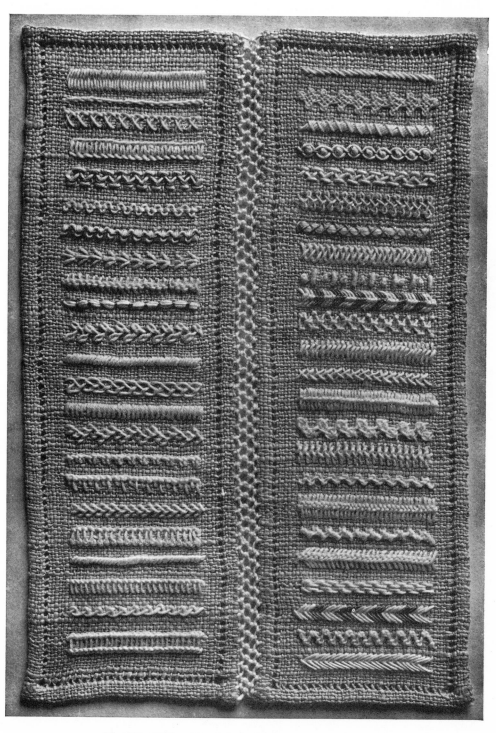

PLATE VIII. Line Stitches (for names see previous page).

PLATE IX.   KNOTS AND CHAINS.   Flowers in Rosette Chain.   Knots in Zig-zag Chain, Knotted Chain and Knotted
Cable Chain.   Dividing lines in Twisted Chevron.   Margin in Chevron.   Trefoils on Bands in Detached Knotted Cable Chain.

ing, or to soften the hard edge of a leaf outline, also as the element in a powder pattern, for dotting regularly over the surface of a leaf. To execute a stitch, bring the thread through at the place where the point of the needle is seen emerging. Pass it to the back at point A and bring it to the surface at point B. A slanting stitch, which should be left a little slack, will have been formed upon the material. Pass the needle and thread under this stitch in the direction from above downwards, and then pass the thread through to the back at point C. In the diagram the needle is completing one stitch and passing the thread along to the point for commencing a fresh one.

ROPE STITCH, figure 50.—This stitch is executed in almost identical fashion to Twisted Chain (figure 57), but, owing to being worked more closely together, is quite different in effect. The only difference in the appearance between this stitch and Satin

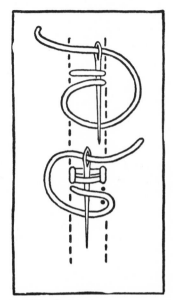

FIG. 48. DIAMOND STITCH.

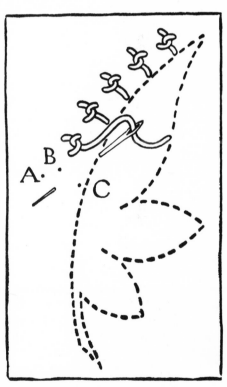

FIG. 49. SWORD-EDGING STITCH.

is that Rope is slightly raised on one side. This slight difference, however, is quite noticeable when the stitch is worked upon spiral lines or tendrils, and it is for purposes of this kind that it is used to best advantage. To work Rope stitch bring the thread through just below the traced line, then insert the needle above the traced line a little farther back and bring it through again at a point close to and just ahead of where it first came through. The needle and thread should now be in the position which is shown in the diagram. Pull the needle through over the working thread and the first stitch is complete. Repeat the process for all succeeding stitches, always inserting and bringing out the needle very close to the last stitch, otherwise the twist of the thread underneath, which raises the stitch, will peep through and spoil the effect.

SCROLL STITCH, figure 51.—A simple decorative line is made by Scroll stitch. It can be worked either in single or double rows or be employed as a filling. A number of rows together might be used to represent flowing water, for the undulating lines of the stitch somewhat suggest this motion. To execute it, bring the thread through at the left-hand end of the traced line. Now form a loop with the working thread by throwing it first towards the right and then back to the starting-point, where it must be held secure by the left thumb. Insert the needle on the traced line in the centre of the loop as shown in the diagram. Pull the loop that now lies under the needle tightly round it, and then pull the thread through to complete the stitch. The best results are gained by working in stout firm thread.

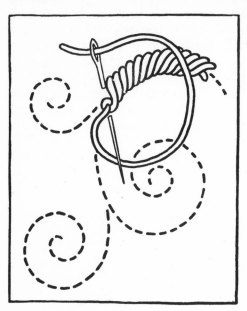

FIG. 50. ROPE STITCH.

PEARL STITCH, figure 52.— When worked closely and with fairly coarse thread this stitch somewhat resembles a row of pearls. Working thus is perhaps the most effective treatment, though another way is to make a jagged line of it by spacing the knots farther apart. This is a useful stitch for executing geometrical patterns in outline, such as, for example, interlacing knot work. To commence, bring the thread through at the right-hand end of a traced line, insert the needle a little to the left just above the traced line and bring it through immediately below, not picking up much material during the process. Pull the thread through and a short slanting stitch will have been laid upon the material. Pass the needle and thread under this slanting stitch in the

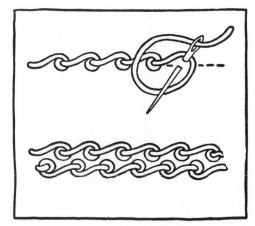

FIG. 51. SCROLL STITCH.

direction from above downwards and do not let it dip into the material on its passage through. (See figure in right-hand diagram, where for the sake of clearness the first part of the stitch is loosened.) Draw the thread through and the first stitch will be complete. In the left-hand figure the entire process of working one stitch and a half of the next one can be followed. In order to obtain the correct appearance the first stage of the stitching should be tightly pulled, and the after threading through left a little loose. This effect is attained by working in the following manner. Leave the first stage of the stitching loose, as seen in the diagram where the needle is at work, until the thread is nearly all passed through it, then tug the thread so as to tighten up the first part of the

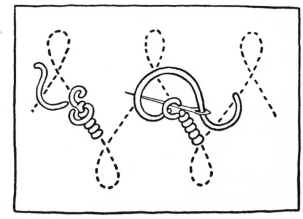

FIG. 52. PEARL STITCH.

stitching, now complete this first part of the stitch by pulling the rest of the thread through and work the second stage of it more loosely.

CHAPTER IV—CHAINED STITCHES

THE chained stitches are a comprehensive group. Beginning with the simple looped Chain, and Split, a form of the same stitch, they develop through various stages of complexity till one like Plaited Braid is obtained which is, perhaps, the most intricate Chain in use.

FIG. 52A. CHAIN STITCH EMBROIDERY.

For the execution of solid fillings, no stitch gives a more refined effect than Split or Chain. Practically the whole of the silk work upon our famous mediæval English embroidery was carried out in this. It works either features or drapery to perfection. It builds up a smooth, even surface, and yet the lines of stitching are just sufficiently distinct to make the modelling of features or drapery clearly evident. For line shading, such as that illustrated in figure 3, Chain answers better than Stem. Perhaps the finest examples of this type of work are to be found on the Dutch East Indian embroideries of seventeenth century date. From one of these, figure 52A has been drawn and figure 52B is a larger detail taken from the same example. The naïve meandering irresponsibility of the designs of this Oriental school, which however are under perfect control and fulfil their purpose with such easy assurance, may be seen in these examples.

FIG. 52B. FRAGMENT FROM A DUTCH EAST INDIAN SEVENTEENTH CENTURY EMBROIDERY.

CHAIN STITCH, figure 53.—The diagram illustrates the working of Chain. For each successive stitch the needle picks up a small, like-sized piece of ground material, each time entering where it last came out and keeping carefully to the traced line. If the stitch is worked correctly a neat line of back stitches should be visible upon the reverse side. Care must be taken not to pucker the ground material and to keep the working regular, for in its monotonous, even appearance lies the beauty of this stitch. For lines or fillings it is equally good and, like any other form of chain, it is especially adapted to the execution of curved or spiral lines. (See Plate X.) DETACHED CHAIN STITCHES, figure 54.—These are useful. They sometimes represent flower petals as in the diagram. Another adaptation is to powder single stitches at regular intervals over a surface to form a light filling. They can be used in the place of isolated French knots, for they are easier to execute and more durable when in use.

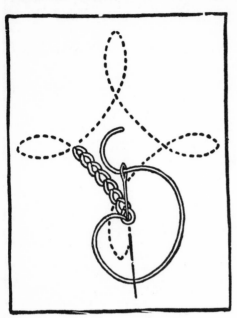

FIG. 53. CHAIN STITCH.

ZIGZAG CHAIN STITCH, figure 55.—This popular stitch consists of a line of ordinary Chain, each loop of which is worked at an angle to the one before. The working is explained by the diagram. A point to be

FIG. 54. DETACHED CHAIN STITCHES.

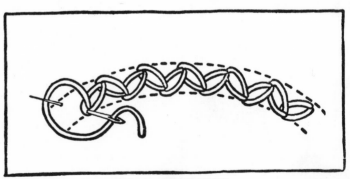

FIG. 55. ZIGZAG CHAIN.

noted is that the needle should, just as it enters the material for each fresh stitch, pierce the end of the loop of the previous stitch. This makes the working more secure. A French knot, placed in the triangle formed by the zigzag treatment of the chain, makes a pretty finish to the line. Stitches such as this make satisfactory edgings to floral designs, for the contrast of the geometrical margin to the more naturalistic form which it encloses is effective. A knot carried out in Zigzag Chain can be seen in the centre of Plate IX.

CHEQUERED CHAIN STITCH, figure 56.—This, a fanciful variety of the ordinary Chain, makes a decorative line of chequered colour. It is executed by means of two strands of silk which are threaded into the needle together. Colours should be chosen which contrast well, though in all other ways the two threads should be similar. To work Chequered Chain, commence as if for the ordinary stitch, but thread two strands in the needle, say dark blue and gold. Upon reaching the stage when

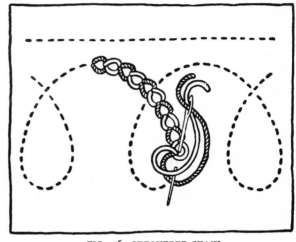

FIG. 56. CHEQUERED CHAIN.

the needle is about to be pulled through over the threads, which should now be lying under it, release one of the threads, say the gold one, from

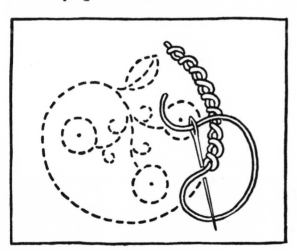

FIG. 57. TWISTED CHAIN.

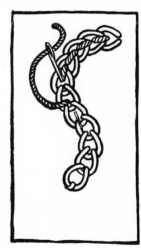

FIG. 58. BACK STITCHED CHAIN.

underneath and let it lie on top of the needle (see needle in figure). Then pull the needle through over the dark blue alone. This will form a Chain loop comprised of the darker coloured thread. Probably some of the gold thread is in evidence upon the surface of the material at the starting-point. It can be disposed of by a gentle pull at this thread. The second stitch is worked in the same way, but this time the gold thread is left looped under the needle and the blue one kept on top. The stitches look best of an equal size, but it is not necessary to make them recur alternately, one light, one dark. Three in succession could be light and then one dark or any other sequence could be followed.

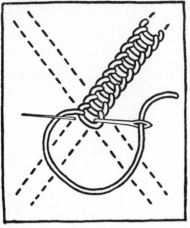

FIG. 59. OPEN CHAIN.

TWISTED CHAIN, figure 57.—This makes a pretty line for stems, curves, and leaf outlines. It is not so definitely linked as the ordinary variety, which may be an advantage. To commence, bring the needle through at the apex. Then hold down the thread near its start towards the left with the thumb, and throw the remainder of the thread over to the right. Next insert the needle in the material just below the starting-point and a little to the left of it. Bring it through lower down in the manner shown by the needle in the figure. The needle is pulled through over the worked thread and this completes the first stitch.

BACK STITCHED CHAIN, figure 58.—A pretty addition to the ordinary Chain is to work a Back stitch down the centre in a contrasting colour. The diagram illustrates this. Treated thus Chain makes a decorative marginal line.

OPEN CHAIN, figure 59.—Narrow bands of this stitch are seen sometimes upon Indian work. In the figure it is being worked upon a straight line, but it can easily be adapted to leaves and other forms of varying width, for with Open Chain it is as simple to follow a broadening outline as a regular one. For the working, bring the thread through on the left-hand traced line, then pass it to the back on the right-hand one opposite the first point, and bring it through again on the other line a little below. The loop is formed by pulling the needle through over the working thread. The loop last worked must be left to lie a little loose upon the ground, for the needle has now, for the second stitch, to enter the material on the right-

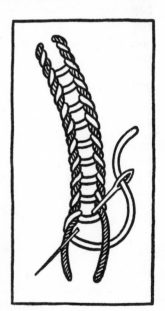

FIG. 60. SINGALESE CHAIN.

hand traced line inside it, and this would not be practicable unless the loop was loose. (See diagram.) Sometimes the stitches lie so close that no ground stuff shows between the transverse threads. This variety can be used to couch down a bunch of threads of contrasting colour. It is quite easy to work the stitch over them.

PLATE X.   PORTION OF *WINDOW BLIND WORKED ON TRANSPARENT
FABRIC*, in Chain, Buttonhole and Double Back Stitches.

PLATE XI. THE JUNGLE. Tree stem in Plaited Braid. Circle in Sheaf. Animal fillings in Lace stitches.

SINGALESE CHAIN, figure 60.—This stitch, a development of Open Chain, is found upon the traditional embroideries of Ceylon. The addition to the ordinary Open Chain consists in a coloured thread being twisted in and out along each edge. To master the stitch, the novice should first learn Open Chain, and then attempt this. To work Singalese Chain, trace two lines upon the material. These traced lines may be two parallel ones or they may be the curved sides of a leaf (figure 61). To execute the stitch, bring through two threads of dark coloured silk. Let one end of each thread emerge at the start of each of the traced lines. These threads should lie upon the surface of the material, and if more convenient let them be pinned down loosely in place upon the traced lines a few inches below. Then for working the chain, bring the light-coloured thread through on the left traced line, just below the start and inside the darker thread. Next pass the working thread underneath the two laid threads in the direction from left to right, and then insert the needle on the traced line opposite

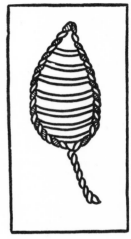

FIG. 61. LEAF IN SINGA-LESE CHAIN.

where it has just come through, and upon the inner side of the dark thread which lies there. Bring the needle to the surface on the opposite traced line and pull it through in the manner illustrated by the needle in the diagram. For each fresh stitch repeat the process.

BROAD CHAIN, figure 62.—A glance at the diagram will show that this is worked in different fashion from the usual stitch. This Chain is firmer and has a tightly plaited appearance which for some purposes is better. To obtain the right effect it is necessary to work with thick thread and take small stitches, otherwise the stitch may resemble ordinary Chain. To work Broad Chain, bring the needle and thread through at the commencement of

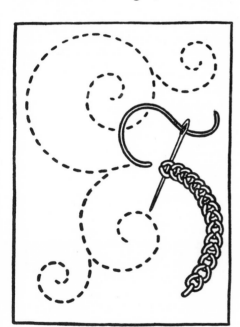

FIG. 62. BROAD CHAIN.

the traced line. Take a short running stitch and bring the needle through again as if for a second, but, instead of taking another, pass the needle under the first stitch and take it to the back again at the point where it last came through. Thus the first loop of the Chain is formed. Bring the needle to the front again upon the traced line a step farther along, and then pass it as before under the stitch behind it, which this time is a Chain loop. When passing the needle under the stitch do not pick up any ground material.

HEAVY CHAIN, figure 63.—This, a similar variety to Broad Chain, is worked in the same backwards fashion, but it is a heavier stitch and makes a bold decorative line suitable for thick stems and other purposes. To execute Heavy Chain first work a Chain loop in the manner described for Broad Chain. Next pass the needle a second time under the first run-stitch in the same way as before, take it to the back at the point where it last came through, and bring it to the surface a short distance farther along the line as with the first stitch. There should now be two Chain loops formed upon the material, a larger one encircling a smaller one, and

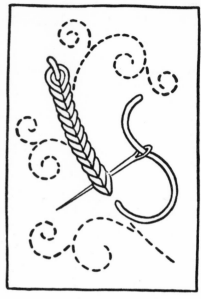

FIG. 63. HEAVY CHAIN.

both passing under the run-stitch. These can be seen in correct position at the starting point in figure 63. The needle in the diagram shows how to continue. Instead of passing the needle back, under the last Chain loop, as it was done for Broad Chain, the needle passes the thread back far enough to pass under the last two Chain loops as it is doing in the diagram.

DOUBLE CHAIN STITCH, figure 64.—This variation upon the common Chain was used in mediæval German linen work. The execution is thus—work

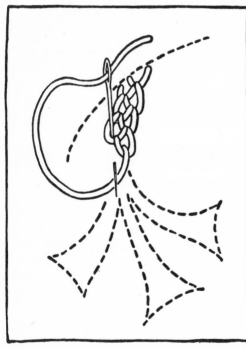

FIG. 64. DOUBLE CHAIN.

an Open Chain loop and into this another one, placing it to the left of the first. Next insert the needle a second time into the centre of the first Chain loop and bring it out below, but on the right side. Pull the needle through over the working thread. For the fourth stitch, throw the thread across to the left and insert the needle in the centre of the second Chain loop, to the left of the thread which is already emerging from this point, and pull it through immediately below ; this stage is illustrated by the needle in the diagram. The process just described is repeated alternately upon either side of the form to be covered, and thus is built up the double row of Chain.

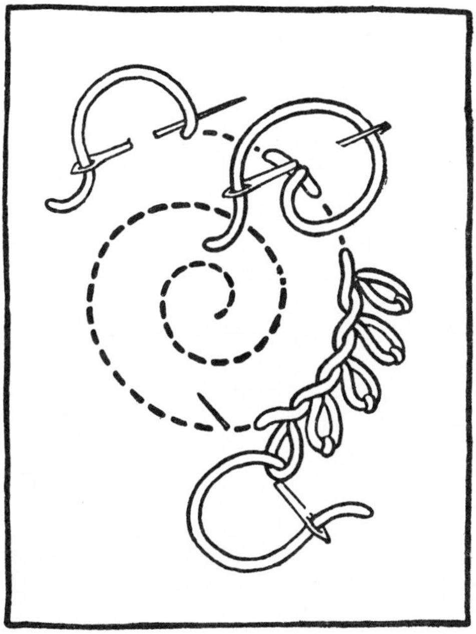

PETAL STITCH, figure 65.—This line stitch is useful for scrolling stems, and it can be used, worked in circular fashion, to represent a small flower. To commence, bring the needle through a quarter of an inch beyond the start of the traced line. Insert it at the beginning and bring it to the surface an eighth of an inch farther along. The uppermost needle is carrying out this first stage, and for the second stage look at the second needle.

FIG. 65. PETAL STITCH.

Here a Single Chain stitch is in process of being formed ; this should lie at a tangent to the traced line. The third stage is shown by the lowest needle. After taking the short stitch which fixes down the Chain loop, the needle is brought through on the traced line, sufficiently far along to be in position for commencing a second stitch similar to the first. To execute this second one the needle enters the material at the base of the just completed Chain loop and emerges at the point on the traced line where the last stitch ended. It should now be in position for forming the next Chain loop.

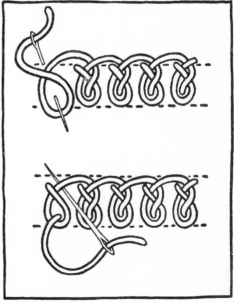

FIG. 66. ROSETTE CHAIN AS A LINE STITCH.

ROSETTE CHAIN, figure 66.—This, as the name implies, is a useful stitch for working small flowers. For a neat finish to collar or cuff, to edge a circle, or for placing upon the margins of a band design, it would be well applied. To work it, bring the needle through at the right-hand end of the upper traced line. Pass the thread across to the left side and hold it down loosely upon the material with the left thumb. Insert the needle as shown in the upper part of the diagram and pull the thread through over the loop. Next pass it under the thread as in the lower diagram, and then proceed to make another stitch a little farther along the line. (See diagram 67.)

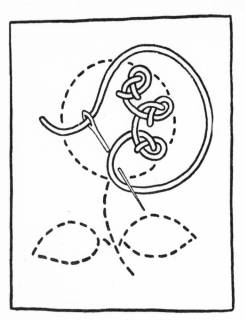

FIG. 67. ROSETTE CHAIN.

ROSETTE CHAIN WORKED UPON A FLOWER, figure 67.— A fairly coarse, twisted thread should be used for this, and if there is a certain stiffness in it, such as is given by glazing, so much the better, for this gives more spring to the curves. When repeated at short intervals round the circumference of a circle, an attractive, conventional representation of a daisy is produced. For the petals to look well, each stitch should, when complete, radiate from a point exactly in the centre of the flower. The stitches can be near together or far apart as suits the subject. Rosette chain is effectively worked in a white thread on a ground of deeper tone. It seems to run especially easily along curves and is well suited for the carrying out of geometrical patterns built up of curved lines. It can be seen worked upon the samplers in Plates IX and XXXII.

CRESTED CHAIN, figure 68.—A fanciful variation upon Chain. The first stage of the working is shown in the upper right-hand corner of the figure. Work first an ordinary Chain stitch on the lower line. Then insert the needle on the upper line in the manner illustrated.

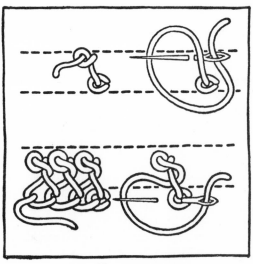

FIG. 68. CRESTED CHAIN.

When the thread is pulled through, a kind of Chain loop or Coral stitch will have been formed on the upper line. Next slip the needle under the slanting thread which joins the two Chain loops and then proceed to work a second Chain stitch on the lower line. The different stages of the working can all be found in the diagram as well as three completed stitches.

BRAID STITCH, figure 69.—Useful for ornamental border lines, this stitch needs a coarse twisted thread to show to advantage. Bring the thread through upon the lower traced line at the right-hand end. Throw the thread across to the left and hold it in place there with the thumb of the left hand. Pass the needle under the held thread in the direction pointing towards the worker. Then twist it round towards the left, passing over the held thread until it points in the opposite direction. The needle should now have the thread twisted round it. Next insert the needle upon the upper traced line a little towards the left, and bring it through again on the lower traced line exactly beneath. The position should now be the one figured

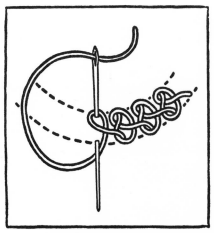

FIG. 69. BRAID STITCH.

in the diagram. If at this point the thread is loose upon the needle, pull it tighter and then draw through. The drawing through may be easier to manage if the left thumb is placed lightly upon the stitch in process of making.

CABLE CHAIN, figure 70.—This is one of the fancy stitches that many workers find attractive. In the diagram the two dotted lines suggest that some other stitch should be worked on either side. Bring the thread through at the apex. With the thumb of the left hand, hold it down loosely upon the material below the starting-point and a little to the right. Next pass the needle under the held thread in the direction from left to right and pass the thread through until only a small loop is left lying upon the material. Insert the needle in the centre of this loop, release the held-down thread and bring the needle through to the surface a little below where it entered and outside the loop. Take hold of the working thread with the right hand and pull it, in order to tighten the loop that is now upon the needle, and then pass the thread round, under the point of the needle, and lay it upon the material upon the left side

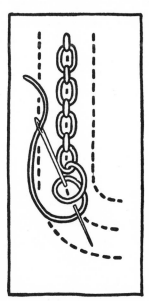

FIG. 70. CABLE CHAIN.

(see diagram). Next place the left thumb lightly upon the stitch in process of making and pull the thread through. The first two links of the chain will have now been made. The first loop can be made by a twist of the needle round the thread and it is the quicker way of the two.

ZIGZAG CABLE CHAIN, figures 71, 72.—A pretty variation is to work Cable in zigzag fashion instead of straight. The difference in working it thus instead of in the ordinary way is that the needle does not pick up a piece of material in a continuous straight line, but each stitch must be taken at an angle to the previous one. This is explained by figure 72, which shows the appearance of the underside of a piece of fabric which has a line of each way of working the stitch upon it.

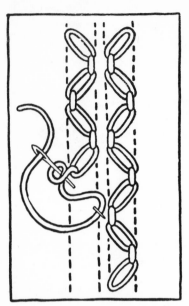

WHEAT-EAR STITCH, figure 73.— Commence at the top of the traced line and work two straight stitches at an angle to each other. Then bring the needle through upon the traced line a little lower down, and pass it under the base of the two single stitches (see diagram), not necessarily letting it enter the material during this process. Take it to the back at the point upon the traced line where it last emerged. This will form a Chain loop and complete the first stitch. The three detached stitches seen in the lower part of the diagram suggest a pretty way to use

FIG. 71. ZIGZAG CABLE CHAIN.

Wheat Ear. Worked thus, the detached stitches, resembling winged seeds, can be used as the repeating

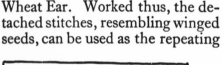
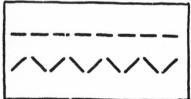

FIG. 72. UNDER SIDE OF THE TWO CABLE CHAINS.

element of a powder pattern over any required surface.

PLAITED BRAID STITCH, figure 74.—As this stitch is perhaps not so simple as some, a detailed diagram has been drawn. The worker may find that to study

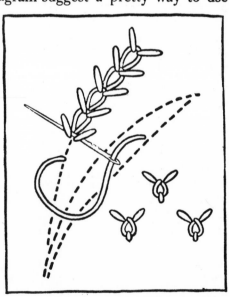

FIG. 73. WHEAT-EAR STITCH.

this diagram is the simplest way to master it. Five successive stitches are there depicted; after working the fifth, glance at stage four for information concerning the succeeding stitch, and then to continue, repeat these last two stages in alternation. To begin, bring the needle through on the left side of the proposed band of stitching. Pass the thread under itself so as to form a loop on the surface of the material; then insert the needle in the centre of this loop, bring it through on the outside of it, and pull the thread through over the working thread (see stage one). For the next development the needle passes the thread under the two threads that cross on the surface (stage two), but it does not enter the material at all this time. For the third movement the needle enters the material and comes out again in the centre of the loops, as illustrated in stage three. For the fourth stitch the needle passes the thread under the crossed threads on the surface, and again does not enter the material; it is simply a repetition of stage two. Stage five is a repetition of stage three, and needs no further description. It will be seen that there are only two different movements, and they occur in alternation; the needle passes the thread in a horizontal direction, alternately, either under the crossed threads or through the loops and the material. Upon the back of the material there should be a row of horizontal stitches equally spaced apart and of the same size. Points to be careful with, are, to leave the loops sufficiently loose to be practicable, and to pick up just the same amount of material each time. The stitch should be worked with coarse stiff thread, and is

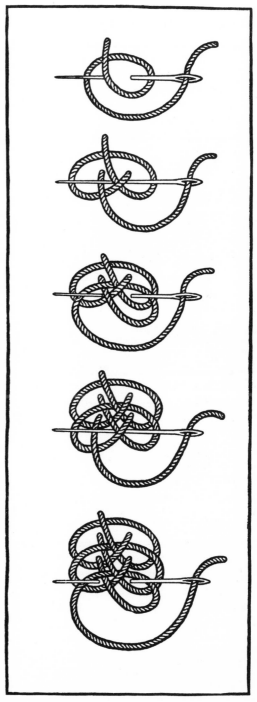

FIG. 74. PLAITED BRAID STITCH.

easily manipulated with metal thread. It is often seen in old **work** executed in gold thread, which is certainly well suited to it both from a practical and a decorative point of view. A large proportion of the thread is on the surface compared to what is underneath, which, from an economical aspect, is important with expensive material. Also it is not wise to draw metal thread to and fro through fabric more than can be helped, and with this stitch there is the minimum amount of it. In Plate XI the stem of the tree is worked in Plaited Braid and it occurs in Plate XXXIII.

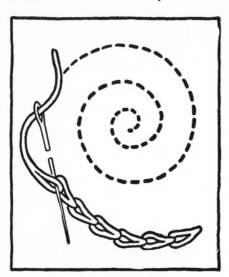

SPLIT STITCH, figure 75.—This can be used either as a line stitch or for solid fillings, it is perhaps especially well adapted to the latter purpose. Split is more used as a frame stitch than for working in the hand. Untwisted silk is the most suitable thread to employ, and if the work is fine a single tress can be divided up into many parts. With Split stitch fillings the direction of the lines of stitching is of importance, for although each individual line does not detach itself from the surrounding ones, yet the direction of the whole mass of lines is plainly evident. A Split stitch

FIG. 75. SPLIT STITCH.

filling is beautifully smooth and flat when well worked, and by the help of this stitch shading can be excellently carried out. Shading in Split does not require to be finely graduated, fairly distinct bands of different tone look the best. The execution is simple to describe, but a certain amount of practice is necessary for good technique. The needle has to pierce the working thread at a point near to where it emerges from the background; this process can be seen in the working diagram. Single lines of Split stitch, worked in fairly coarse silk or wool, are often employed to represent stems, and another common use is to lay a line of Split stitch beside couched lines of gold or silver

FIG. 76. HEAD FROM MEDIÆVAL EMBROIDERY.

thread. In English mediæval embroidery this stitch was employed for practically all the silk work. Figure 76, a head of Christ drawn from the cope preserved at S. Bertrand de Comminges, shows the direction taken by the lines of Split stitch in order to express the drawing of features and hair.

PLATE XII. THE WAYSIDE. Fence in Chevron. Gate in Chequered Chain
Band. Hedgehog in Bullion Knots. Trellis upon snail, beetle and strawberry.
Centre flower in Detached Overcast. Shell and caterpillar in Buttonhole.

PLATE XIII. THE MEADOW. *Lamb in Trellis. Sheep in French Knots. Other animals and tree trunks in regular Stem. Leaves in Detached Buttonhole. Background in Open Buttonhole. Marginal lines in Chequered Chain Band. Double Back and Raised Chained Band.*

CHAPTER V—KNOTTED STITCHES

THE knotted stitches form a distinct group of great interest both historically and technically. The irregular texture that they give to the surface of the material is useful in making a pleasant contrast to the smoothness of the flat stitches. One or other form of Knot stitch can be used for line work, solid or open fillings, detached elements or edgings. That the decoration of large hangings can be successfully carried out solely by the aid of French Knots has been clearly proved by the Chinese workers. One stitch of this group, Trellis (figure 87), claims attention, for until its recent revival it appears to have fallen into disuse since the sixteenth and seventeenth centuries, when it was commonly found upon English work. It is an ingeniously designed stitch, extremely useful for solid fillings. By working it in different ways distinct effects can be obtained which can be seen in Plates XII, XIII, XIV, XVIII.

FRENCH KNOTS, figure 77.—To be satisfactory, knots must be neat and firm, or they will move out of place at the slightest provocation, and be loose and irregular. They are most frequently used massed together, as in the centres of flowers, and they keep in position best when packed close in this fashion. Detached knots, however, are valuable for decorative purposes. A row of them, separated each from the other by just the space occupied by one, makes a pretty finish round the outside of a leaf, or upon the sides of border lines. The diagram illustrates a French Knot in the making. To commence, bring the thread through at the required place. Hold it tautly with the thumb and finger of the left hand, about an inch and a half distant from the place where it came through. Let the point of the needle encircle the held thread twice (see diagram), and then, with the twists upon the point kept fairly tight by still holding firmly on to the thread, revolve the needle round until the point of it is close to where the thread first came through. Now pass the needle and thread through the twists to the back of the material. The completed knot, if well made, will resemble a bead laid endways up upon the material. French Knots can be executed in the hand or the frame ; they are most perfectly executed with the aid of the latter, for then both hands are free for manipulation. When they are made in the hand, the material has to be held, during the process of making, between the second and third finger of the left hand, as the thumb and first finger must be free for holding the thread. One, two, or three twists can be placed upon the needle according to the required size of knot.

FOUR-LEGGED KNOT STITCH, figure 78.—To work the simple stitch illustrated here, bring the thread to the surface at the required place, insert the needle about one-eighth of an inch above the starting point and bring it through again on the right-hand side, as illustrated in the upper left-hand figure in the diagram. Next, throw the working thread across to the left and hold it down there upon the material with the thumb. Then pass the needle underneath the point where the thread crosses the first stitch; do not let it pierce the fabric below, and pull it through as shown in the lowest figure in the diagram. Take the thread to the back so that the fourth support to the knot is in correct position. A completed knot can be seen in the right-hand corner. This stitch makes a neat device for powdering a lightly filled surface. For such a purpose these little knots can either be thrown down

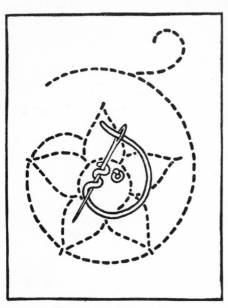

FIG. 77. FRENCH KNOTS.

haphazard, the legs pointing in all directions, or be laid in regular rows, but in either case they should be spaced fairly evenly apart.

BULLION KNOT, figure 79.—This stitch is composed of a tightly coiled spiral of thread which is fixed to the surface by a thread passing through its centre and entering the material at either extremity. There is a certain knack in the making, and until practice discovers this, the stitch is a little tiresome to manage. Whatever the working thread consists of there should be substance in it, otherwise the knot will be thin and poor, instead of full and round. The needle should be thick and its eye not much broader

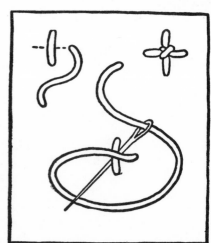

FIG. 78. FOUR-LEGGED KNOT STITCH.

than the other part, for one of this kind slips easily through the coil of twists upon it. In the diagram the Knot is being used to work both flower petals and leaves of a small sprig. More often, massed together, the knots are used to fill in the centres of flowers. To work the stitch, bring the thread to the surface near the centre of the flower. Insert the needle on the outer edge and bring it through again at the exact point where it first came out. The needle should be pushed as far through the stuff as possible in order that the twists, which are now to be put upon it, should be wound round its thicker end rather than the point. Next wind the thread seven or eight times around the needle close to where it emerges from the material, and then place the thumb lightly upon the coils now formed. Then pull the thread through. When it is as tight as it will come, pass the needle and thread over, so that they point in the opposite direction. This lays the knot in its correct place. Now again tighten the thread as the changed position will have made it a little slack. Pass the thread to the back at the point where it first went through. The knot is now complete and should resemble a small caterpillar laid upon the surface. The knots may vary in length. The needle usually

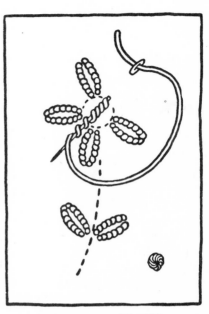

FIG. 79. BULLION KNOT.

picks up about one-sixteenth of an inch of ground stuff, and it is necessary to put as many twists upon it as will cover up, with closely packed coils, that amount of space. A handsome knot, sometimes seen on Chinese embroidery, can be made thus : Thread in the needle several strands of untwisted floss silk of distinct colours. When preparing to form the knot, pick up with the needle only a minute piece of material, but put ten or twelve twists of silk upon it. Complete the stitch in the manner described above, and there will have been formed a tightly coiled-up knot. An example of this is

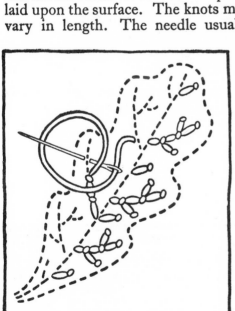

FIG. 80. CORAL STITCH.

illustrated in the lower corner of the diagram.

CORAL STITCH, figure 80.—Coral, like most of the knotted stitches, makes a somewhat irregular, but decorative line. It is often used for the open fillings of large leaves, such as those frequently seen upon the seventeenth-century English wool-work hangings. (See figure 81.) The stitch consists of a knot, which is tied in the thread and at the same action of the needle attached to the material. To work it, bring the

FIG. 81. PORTION OF A JACOBEAN HANGING.

thread through at the right-hand end of a line. Hold the thread down upon the material along the line to be worked. Insert the needle as shown in the diagram and pull it through. Various braiding designs can be prettily carried out with Coral stitch. In England, in the seventeenth century, it was a fashionable pastime with ladies to knot up, with the aid of a netting needle, balls of linen thread. These were afterwards couched down by another thread on to the material, following out some pretty braiding pattern. These couched knotted threads would have much the same appearance as Coral stitch.

ZIGZAG CORAL STITCH, figure 82.—Coral looks well worked in zigzag fashion. Many stitches answer well to this angular treatment. The difference between ordinary Coral and this, is, that here the stitch is carried to and fro and placed alternately upon the left and the right-hand traced line. This zigzag treatment makes quite a decorative band of stitching suitable for borders and other purposes.

DOUBLE KNOT STITCH, figure 83.—This variety makes a larger, more important knot than Coral, effective for all forms of decorative line work. The needle, after bringing the thread through for the start, takes a small slanting stitch passing

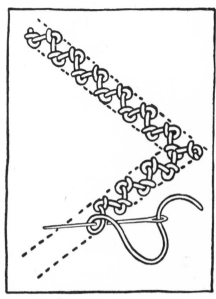

FIG. 82. ZIGZAG CORAL STITCH.

under the traced line (see upper needle in diagram). Next it slips the working thread under the short stitch just formed, and which now lies on the material. Then for a second time it slips the thread under the same stitch, working this time after the manner of buttonholing. These last two processes can be clearly followed where the lower needle is at work. Figure 84 illustrates the same stitch worked in the opposite direction. This diagram shows in more detail the various stages of the working. To gain the right effect with Double Knot stitch, it is necessary to pull the thread tautly at each stage of the working (see Plate XXA).

KNOTTED CHAIN STITCH, figure 85.—Knotted Chain is a bold

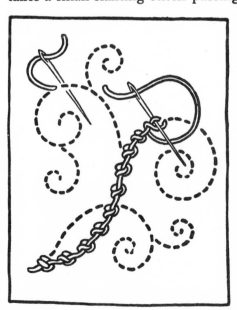

FIG. 83. DOUBLE KNOT STITCH.

decorative stitch, useful for line work. Like most of the fancy stitches it shows to best advantage worked with stout thread. To work it, bring the thread through at the right-hand end of the traced line. Insert

F

the needle about one-sixteenth of an inch farther to the left above the traced line and bring it through below it. The piece of material which would thus be picked up by the needle is illustrated in the diagram by two dots placed just beyond the working needle. Draw the thread through and a short slanting stitch will have been formed upon the surface. Next throw the thread over to the left, hold it down with the thumb and then pass the needle through the slanting stitch just formed, from above downwards, and draw the thread through, leaving it a little slack. Again throw the thread round to the left and hold it under the thumb and then pass the needle and thread through this slack loop (see needle in diagram). When the thread is pulled through the first two links of the chain are made. The dots placed upon either side of the traced line mark the points where the needle should next go through for the con-

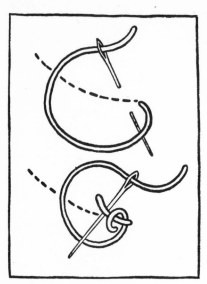

FIG. 84. DOUBLE KNOT STITCH.
(VARIATION.)

tinuation of the stitch. This stitch carries out one of the knots in Plate IX and one in Plate X.

KNOTTED CABLE CHAIN, figure 86.—A pretty stitch, more decorative than the ordinary Cable (figure 70). It is chain-like in character, and therefore suitable for use upon curved lines. In the diagram, the stitch is illustrated in three stages. Bring the needle through to the surface at the right-hand end of the curved line. Proceed to work a Coral stitch close to the starting-point. This can be seen in process where the upper needle is at work. The Coral knot completed, the needle then passes the thread under the stitch just formed, in order to get into correct position for working the next stage. The thread, just passed under, with the loose end emerging, can be seen in the diagram on the worked detail occurring on the left side. The third stage of the execution is illustrated at the point where the lower needle is at work. There the

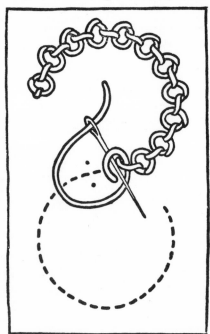

FIG. 85. KNOTTED CHAIN STITCH.

loop of the chain is being formed. Pull the needle through over the working thread. For the second stitch commence by again forming the Coral knot. An example of the use of this stitch can be seen in Plate IX, where the interlaced knot on the left is executed in it. The little scroll design at top and base of this sampler has its berries composed of detached stitches of Knotted Cable Chain. This variety is more effective for such petals than the Common Chain which is more often used for the purpose.

TRELLIS STITCH, figures 87–89.—Though nowadays an almost unknown stitch, Trellis is unusually attractive. It seems to be of English origin and to have been in common use in the middle of the sixteenth century, for it is often seen upon dress embroidery of that period and later upon the earliest known English samplers. Trellis is used for solid fillings. To obtain the correct effect it is especially necessary to have very perfect technique, for any irregularity in the working quite changes its character. The thread for working Trellis stitch should be untwisted for the best effect to be

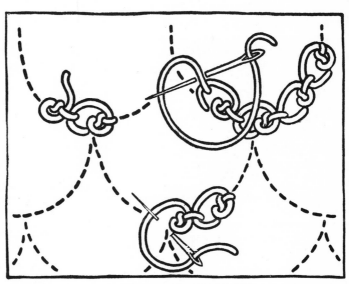

FIG. 86 KNOTTED CABLE CHAIN.

gained. Figure 88 shows various stages in the working. First outline the form with either Chain or Back stitch. This is necessary because Trellis does not enter the ground material at all, wherever it touches the margin it is attached to this outline. Whether Chain or Back is the stitch chosen for use depends upon what effect is required ; with the Chain line half of it shows after the filling is worked and this may be an advantage, for an outline usually gives a finish to a form. In the upper part of figure 88 a portion of Chain outline is illustrated, and where the needle is at work the first stage in the execution can be seen. The thread comes up from the back through the Chain line and the needle is passed upwards through the adjoining stitch. The second stage is shown farther along to the right ; the thread is here being looped through itself and the knot thus formed must next be pulled tight. A knot just completed and the needle passing on to the next stitch can be seen in figure 87, where half a filling has been worked in Trellis. It should be noted that the knots take a slanting direction, and in order to obtain this result it is necessary to pull the thread at the correct angle, at the moment when the knot is nearly tight. The knots are repeated in similar fashion until the end of the line is reached, one being taken into each Chain loop. For the second line of stitching the execution is similar to the first, but owing to its being worked in a contrary direction, from right to left, the looping must also be reversed (see lower line in figure 88). The second and all succeeding lines are worked into the line above them, and it is necessary to make the needle, each time it enters the previous line, enter it at exactly the right point. This is in the space which naturally occurs between one knot and the next, for at this point there is just room for the needle to pass easily through, but any attempt to pierce the knots themselves would be impracticable as well as having the result of putting the new stitch not

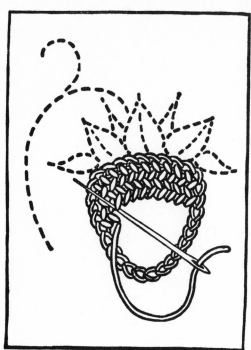

FIG. 87. TRELLIS STITCH.

quite in its right position. The stitch with several rows worked has been illustrated in figure 87 as a filling for a strawberry, a subject it suits particularly well. In this diagram the needle can be seen entering the row above it in correct fashion. It is usual to execute Trellis fillings in straight lines to and fro as shown in the strawberry diagram, but there are other ways of working. The stitch can be executed entirely in one direction, say right to left, and then a pattern of parallel slanting lines will be seen to develop (see right-hand diagram

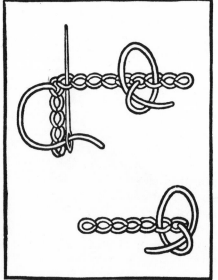

FIG. 88. THE WORKING OF TRELLIS STITCH.

in figure 89). For this method of working, at the end of each row, the thread has to be run back on the underneath of the material in order to be in correct position for starting the fresh line. The left-hand square in figure 89 exhibits a chevron pattern. This can be contrived by

PLATE XIV. THE HARVEST FIELD. Mice in Trellis stitch.
Border in Sheaf, Corn in Feather and Stem. Ground in Buttonhole.

PLATE XV. *Formal Trees and Medallion in Interlacing stitch. Border in Threaded Back.*

working three or more consecutive rows of stitching in one direction and then three in the other and so on. If the chevron requires to be still more marked, the colour or shade of the silk can be changed with each variation in the direction of the stitch. Still another method of working Trellis is illustrated in the centre of this figure. Here the knots are worked round and round in spiral form, commencing at the centre. The innermost circle of knots is fixed into a Single Chain stitch and the spiral is continued until the requisite sized disc is obtained. With this form of Trellis it is necessary occasionally to work two knots in succession into one hole, otherwise the surface will not remain flat. Spiral Trellis is useful for centres of flowers ; they may be worked in actual position or separately on another piece of material. In the latter case, in order to release them, cut the threads of the material near by where the Single Chain stitch has been attached. This frees the disc and it can then be applied to the flower centre and fixed in place by a neat hemming round its edge to the base of the petals. The final row of any Trellis filling is always attached to its outline by this means. When filling in forms like petals it often becomes necessary to decrease the number of stitches towards the base ; it is not advisable either to increase or to decrease the knots at any point excepting at the extremities of lines. A new thread should be started at the commencement of a row, not in the middle, for it needs

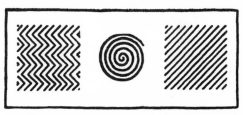

FIG. 89. THE DIRECTION OF THE KNOTTED LINES IN TRELLIS.

very deft fingers to manage it invisibly at any other part. To look their best the knots should not be pulled too tightly or the silky effect may be lost, also they should lie just nicely together, not too close nor too far apart. The mass of stitching should lie perfectly flat and even ; if too many stitches are put in the surface will bulge. Sometimes, however, raised effects of various kinds are deliberately aimed at. A flower centre is often effective worked in a half-sphere form and this is easily contrived by means of Spiral Trellis. Semi-detached petals, which are quaint and pretty, are also easily worked by the help of this stitch ; it is quite one of the best for the purpose. Trellis in its different forms occurs in Plates XII, XIII, XIV, XVa, XVIII and XXa.

HOLLIE STITCH, figure 90.—Though famous as a lace stitch, this is a useful variety for fine embroidery. It lends itself to colour work admirably, and can be used in delicate treatments of petals, centres, and calices of flowers. It is seen in use upon the fine seventeenth-century English samplers. In construction it is like Buttonhole stitch, but with an extra twist added. First outline a small square with a fine, close Chain. Then bring the working thread through on the upper right side of the square to be worked, in the centre of a Chain loop. (See larger arrow in diagram.) Next, carry the thread across to the opposite side, pass it to the back, and bring it up through the centre of the Chain loop opposite the other (see smaller arrow). Then place the left thumb near the start, upon the working thread as it lies upon the material in position for forming an ordinary Buttonhole stitch. With the right hand, which now holds the needle and thread in readiness to continue, pass the working thread once round the left thumb in direction from right to left. Then continue as for Buttonhole stitch, by passing the needle into the row of Chain above, and bringing it down under the laid thread and through the loop now encircling the thumb. (See diagram.) Draw the thread through and the first stitch will be complete. Upon reaching the end of a line, throw the thread again across from right to left and continue as before, but working into the heading of the last row, instead of into the Chain line. As workers in Hollie Point lace know, patterns in this stitch can be built up by different arrangements of the spacing of the stitches. Sometimes even verses of poetry and dates are cleverly shown up in lettering simply by this means. For the omission of a stitch or stitches causes a space to be left, which shows up as a dark square against the light ones filled with solid stitches. It is thus that letters or a pattern can be built up. This patterning of the surface when working Hollie stitch is more suited for lace than for embroidery. A single knot of larger size has been

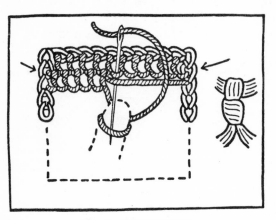

FIG. 90. HOLLIE STITCH.

placed at the right of the working figure. This shows more clearly than the other part how the knot loops itself into the row above, also the twist around the neck of the loop.

TURK'S HEAD KNOT, figure 91.—When making up work, it is useful to know how to decorate it with fringes, balls, and tassels. A pretty ball for such a purpose is illustrated in the diagram. A completed ball is shown in the lower portion and the way to start the making of it, above. At first the making seems intricate, but practice soon overcomes this. One of the secrets of success lies in using suitable thread. This must be of a firm, stout and rather wiry nature. To begin, arrange the thread in a kind of double loop, just as seen in the diagram. Hold this arrangement of loops at the base between the left-hand finger and thumb, and then pass the needle in and out of them as shown. Before finally pulling the needle through, tighten up the loops a little whilst they are around it, for at first they are usually too large for the completed ball. This knot in the diagram, with the needle through it, represents the framework, or skeleton, of the future ball, and it should take up about the same area as the ball will, when complete. It is only by experience that the novice can learn the correct size for the start.

She must be content to make the first ball perhaps a little loosely welded together instead of tightly knotted up like the sample ones in Plate XXXIII. After the original loops have been tightened up, the needle pulls the thread through them and then proceeds to continue threading in and out of the partly formed ball, by following the lead started by the dotted line in the diagram. This entails exactly following the lead of the original thread from start to finish, passing over and under the various loops, as it does. This threading in and out continues until three rows of thread lie side by side as seen in the completed ball below. Whilst this is proceeding the framework of the ball in process of making must be coaxed between the fingers of the left hand, into taking a rounded sphere form rather than a flat one, for the result aimed at is a ball. If this is not done, there will be an ugly gap at one side of the completed ball, even though it may have been correctly knotted up. Care must be taken, during the making, to keep the needle always on the inside of the thread it is following, otherwise the lines of thread will cross each other instead of lying side by side, and much mar the effect. Possibly one or two trials will be necessary before perfection is attained, but the finished ball is so pretty, it is worth taking the trouble to master its technique.

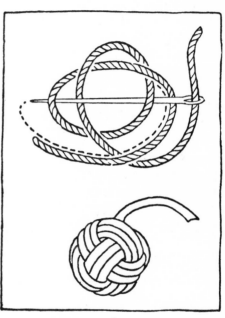

FIG. 91. TURK'S HEAD KNOT.

BALL STITCH, figure 92.—A neat covering for a tassel head or for a ball can be quickly and easily made by this stitch. It is more effective for such a purpose than the Buttonhole so often applied to this use. In the diagram the correct way to commence is shown, as well as the first stitch. A loop must be formed round the apex of the ball, by tying a loose knot in the working thread exactly like that in the diagram. The loose end and knot are made both secure and tighter later on, when the stitches are worked over them ; meanwhile the left thumb can be kept upon the knot to keep it together. Now proceed to make the first stitch upon the loop as shown in the diagram. When the thread is pulled through, continue to work round the loop a series of similar stitches, fairly close together, until the starting-point is again reached. The second and succeeding rows of stitches are worked into the previous row and care must be taken that only one comes between each stitch of the row above. As the circumference of the circle of stitches grows wider, the number of stitches in each row must not increase; they must be spaced wider apart in order to cover the greater area, and later on, be gathered closer together again, as the lower part of the ball is being covered. If the stitch is carried out correctly, a geometrical pattern of diagonal lines is formed upon the ball. Stout linen thread suits the stitch better than soft silk. A simple and practical way to make the padding for a ball or tassel head is—take a narrow strip of soft linen, say, a quarter of an inch wide, and tapering to one-eighth at one end, and, starting with the wider end, roll it up. Work the stitch around, but not into this stuffing—the right moment to put the padding in place is when half the cover is completed. When the covering of the ball is completed, the needle passes the remaining portion of the working thread up through the centre of the ball and out at the top where it will be found useful for fixing the ball in place.

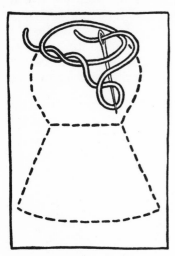

FIG. 92. BALL STITCH.

ANTWERP EDGE, figure 93.—The diagram illustrates a simple knotted stitch useful for working an ornamental edge. It would be most effective carried out in stout, rather than in soft, thread. To begin, the thread must be made firm at the left-hand end of the line, then the needle passes it through the edge of the material in the direction from above downwards. Next, upon the loop thus formed, a kind of Buttonhole stitch is worked (see needle in diagram). This ties a firm knot, and completes the stitch.

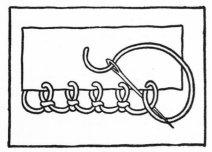

FIG. 93. ANTWERP EDGE.

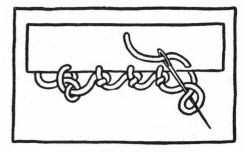

FIG. 94. ARMENIAN EDGE.

ARMENIAN EDGE, figure 94.—A pretty knotted edge is made by this stitch. In the diagram, the first knot is loosened, in order to show its formation. The next three are complete and the fifth is in process of being worked. The needle is just about to pull the thread through in the correct fashion for tying the knot.

CHAPTER VI—COMPOSITE STITCHES

A LARGE number of stitches belong to this group, and a fine bold type of embroidery has been evolved by their aid. Designs of a conventional nature are best suited to the technique, and fairly large forms with simple outlines show the fillings to best advantage. These fillings are often made up of a geometrical diapering, and look well carried out in white and natural coloured threads, enclosed by a darker marginal line. (See Sampler XVII.) Coloured work is sometimes successfully achieved by means of these stitches, but as a rule variation of texture and patterned detail is the aim rather than a colour effect. Usually two or more stitches are necessary to their formation. One makes the foundation and the other is frequently a surface interlacement upon it. Many of the stitches, both for lines and fillings, are worked upon preliminary laid bars of thread thrown across from side to side of the form. Upon these bars, stitches such as Stem, Chain, and Cretan, for example, are

FIG. 95. INTERLACING STITCH.

worked, and a bold effect is gained by thus raising them slightly from the ground. Some interesting examples of this type of work come from Italy and Portugal.

INTERLACING STITCH, figures 95-98.—This stitch, so named because it is built up of threads which constantly interlace one with another, is of ancient origin. It is commonly seen on German fourteenth-century white linen work, also carried out in silk thread in colours, upon much Eastern work of later date. It can be used to execute geometrical patterns or for formal floral work. Another useful adaptation is as an insertion stitch, using either a single line of it, or several rows together. For joining strips of embroidery, for piecing up a patchwork of squares, or for any like use it makes a pretty contrast and finish to the rest of the work. For the ornamentation of household linens it is easy to devise simple border patterns, insertions, corners, or centres for working in Interlacing stitch. It is well suited for such objects, and for these a fine white linen thread will usually be best to work with, though sometimes the combination of Delft blue and white is equally effective. For many other purposes the stitch looks extremely well worked in a combination of two colours, either contrasted or harmonised. There are two processes in carrying out Interlacing stitch : a preliminary foundation, and a threading in and out upon it. The final stage of the working is done

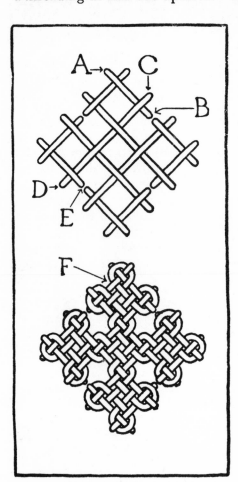

entirely upon a prepared basis formed of the Herringbone, so well known in plain needlework. The first proceeding is to prepare the foundation. Figure 95 is a working diagram illustrating various stages. The foundation consists of two lines of Herringbone, the one imposed upon the other. These differ, however, in one point from the plain needlework form—namely, that as the stitches cross one another they pass over or under in slightly different fashion from usual. For the correct working of the final stage it is imperative that the passing over and under of these foundation threads should be exactly like the samples in the diagram, so after working the first line it will be well to compare it with the copy. Figure 98, which is a diagram of the foundation only, of another pattern for Interlacing stitch, may be of help at this stage of the working, for all are similar in construction. It will be noticed that when the second line of Herringboning is completed the threads now interweave quite regularly, alternately over and under each other, throughout the band. For the final interlacement the thread is brought through to the surface, at the left-

FIG 96. MALTESE CROSS IN INTER-
LACING STITCH.

hand end of the band in the worked diagram. This thread now proceeds to make a series of continuous loops which are worked in and out of the upper half of the Herringbone foundation. Here again the correct overs and unders of the crossing threads must be carefully observed. In figure 95, this threading in and out can be clearly followed. When the end of the line is reached, the thread, in order to return and thus complete the band of stitching, encircles the crossed lines in the centre of the band, and then begins to make a second similar series of loops on the lower half of the Herringbone basis. For this the thread is again twisted in and out of the foundation threads in just the same way as before, only this time it must also interlace correctly with the upper series of loops, which a little further complicates the threading in and out. A simple line of Interlacing stitch having been worked, it will be interesting to discover other slightly more complicated patterns which lend themselves to it. The lower portion of figure 96 exhibits a Maltese cross in this stitch, and above the foundation upon which the final interlacement was worked. This or more complex developments of the same idea make charming elements in a composition. The working should be mastered chiefly by studying the diagrams. The first process is to work the foundation. Bring the thread through at point A (see figure 96), and take it to the back at B. Bring it through again at C, and return it to the back at D. The thread comes through again at E, and the rest of the working can be followed out by studying the

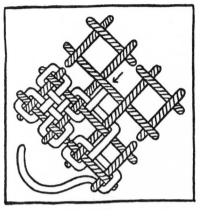

FIG. 97. MALTESE CROSS, PARTLY WORKED.

diagram, for practically the same process is repeated continuously until the figure is completed by taking the thread through to the back exactly opposite the starting-point A. It is important that the interlacing of the threads in this preliminary framework should be correct, so at this point the worker would be wise carefully to compare her work with the diagram. Next the surface interlacing is threaded through. In this part of the work

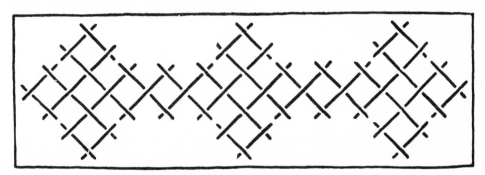

FIG. 98. FOUNDATION FOR WIDE BAND IN INTERLACING STITCH.

the thread hardly enters the ground material. Figure 97 is a drawing of the cross showing the final stage partly worked. The working thread emerges from under one of the foundation threads (see arrow) and its after-wanderings can easily be followed in the figure as it twists in and out, filling in, as far as it has been taken, the interstices of the cross. This final interlacement is worked in practically the same way as for the straight band, only here each diamond shape is completely filled in before passing on to the next, and by passing correctly from one diamond form to another, the worker automatically fills in the diamond shape in the centre. It will be observed that the foundation of the Maltese cross is built up of five of these shapes arranged in form of a cross, and upon glancing at figures 95 and 98, these same shapes are seen, but ranged in line. The basis of any pattern for Interlacing stitch is founded upon different arrangements of this or a similar unit. This knowledge will enable an interested worker to devise any number of fresh patterns. They are most easily drawn out upon squared paper. A number of adaptations of this stitch are illustrated in the samplers. Plate XV contains a circular design in the centre and a tree on either side. The flowers of the tree in Plate XXA are in Interlacing, the foundation being pentagonal. Worked in a simple line it occurs in Plate XXVI, and in Plate XVI the tiny central

flowers are worked in the simplest form of all, just one unit, alternately of diamond or pentagonal form, being used for this foundation. Figure 98 shows the foundation threads of a broad band in Interlacing stitch. Before either drawing out a pattern or choosing a working thread, it is necessary to know that a certain proportion must be kept between the two in order that the final interlacement should fill in the required spaces neatly. If the pattern is on a large scale, the thread must be coarse, and *vice versa*. If the threads are too open the effect is poor ; if they are too close the stitch is tiresome to work, neither does it look so well. For the final stage of the working, a blunt-pointed needle should be used, as the ordinary sharp one

FIG. 99. TWISTED LATTICE STITCH.

is inclined to pierce threads instead of passing clearly over or under them. The preliminary foundation should be rather slackly worked, or it may be drawn up and cause the background to pucker when the surface thread is wound about it. The larger the area covered the more is this likely to happen.

TWISTED LATTICE, figures 99, 100.—This stitch can be worked upon lines, fillings, or cut spaces. In the diagram, twisted lattice is being used to form a semi-open filling upon the surface of a leaf. Sometimes a strip of it is worked, enclosed between two lines. For this, a single line of Herringbone can form the foundation, though more often such a band is based upon a doubling of the herringbone basis. Figure 100 illustrates both these methods. Decorative bands of this stitch used upon stems are commonly to be seen upon old German and Swiss linen embroidery. To work the leaf as in figure 99, begin by laying across a net-work of foundation threads. Lay first all the threads in one direction, then the

PLATE XVI. KNOT WORK in Pekinese. Rosettes in Interlacing. Parts of ground in Faggot stitch.

PLATE XVII. FORMAL LEAF TREATMENTS, in Buttonhole and Composite stitches.

opposite ones, and let these be darned in and out of the first set, for when completed the threads of the lattice should regularly interlace over and under each other. This completed, a new thread is taken and twisted in and out in the manner shown in the diagram. The needle passes perpendicularly, up under one transverse thread, then down under the next, and so on till the end of the line is reached. There is no need for a space filled in with twisted lattice to have a background of material behind it; the stitch is used sometimes as a filling for cut or open work like a lace filling. When using it thus, it may be necessary to make a closer network of lattice threads, or the filling might not be sufficiently durable (see Plate XXXIII).

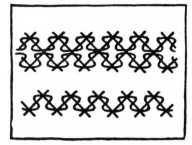

FIG. 100. A BAND OF TWISTED LATTICE.

WHIPPED RUN STITCH, figure 101.— This simple stitch is shown to best advantage when used as a filling, though it can be used for line work. For either coarse or fine embroidery it is equally good. Sometimes fine Indian muslin work is entirely executed in this stitch, with lovely effect. To commence working as in figure 101, run an even line of thread round the margin, making the stitches of even length, and not picking up much ground stuff. The next process is to twist the working thread in and out of the run line. (See needle in diagram.) Run a second line of thread round close to the first and then twist the thread in and out as before. The thread must always twist through in the same direction. The first running must not be too tightly drawn through or the after twisting may make the ground material pucker.

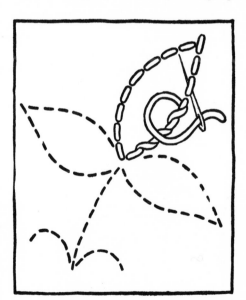

FIG. 101. WHIPPED RUN STITCH.

PEKINESE STITCH, figure 102. This variety is commonly used by Chinese workers for executing entire embroideries, as an alternative to Chain, or knots. It is thought highly of, for an embroidery in Pekinese fetches double the price of one in Chain. Row upon row, in extremely fine shaded stitching, is employed for the fillings of flowers and other forms. It also makes a good line or outline stitch. The central leaf in Plate XXXIII illustrates it thus, for it there forms the outline to the leaf. In Plate XVI the interlacing knot work is entirely carried out in it, it also forms the marginal line in Plate XXVIII. To execute Pekinese, first work a line of close Back stitches and then pass the thread through this foundation, in the manner illustrated in the diagram (figure 102). Here for the sake of clearness, the loops are loosely taken through, but in reality each loop, especially the lower portion of it, is pulled fairly tight. Any succeeding rows should be worked closely above the first. The suit-ability of this stitch for working in metal and other obstinate threads will be at once appreciated. A couched or run line may if necessary be sub-stituted for the Back stitches.

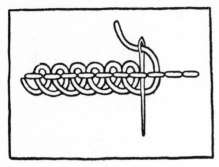

FIG. 102. PEKINESE STITCH.

THREADED BACK STITCH, fig-ure 103.—Some threads are trouble-some to pass through material, and for these it is useful to know of stitches like this one, with which there is little passage to and fro. To commence, work a foundation of Back stitching. The thread for this need not be the same as that for the other part. Other stitches might replace the Back stitch, if preferred, such as, for example, ordinary or fancy Chains, and one like Feather looks well with some threading in and out about its centre. In the diagram, towards the lower right-hand corner, the Back stitch is in process of formation. Opposite, the needle can be seen carrying out the first portion of the threading, and higher up a loose end of thread shows how far the second stage of the threading has been carried. The second stage is a repe-tition of the first and it fills in the vacant spaces between the already finished portion. Used as a decora-tive line the stitch is effective with only one threading in and out. (See border in Plate XV.)

RAISED CHEVRON STITCH, figure 104.—Chevron worked upon a foundation appears bolder in effect than when stitched directly on to the ground fabric. (See figure 19.) The foundation must be properly laid. The thread used for it should not be too fine, but of a soft kind that lies flatly down. The stitches must be of correct size and spaced at the right distance apart. The foundation can

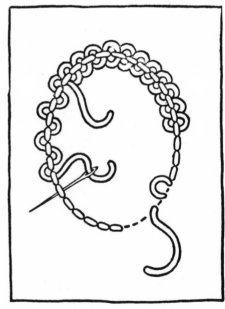

FIG. 103. THREADED BACK STITCH.

be seen in process of execution in the upper line in figure 104. To com-mence, bring the thread through on the centre traced line, insert the needle on the upper line, as in process in the diagram. Draw the thread through and then insert the needle on the centre traced line at the point where it first came through, and bring it to the surface a little farther to the left. Next work a similar wedge below, reversed in position. The needle when working is always horizontal, and by inserting it at exactly the right points, the wedges are correctly laid. In the diagram dots can be seen marking out the continuation. The surface thread is commenced at the left end of the line. The needle winds the thread in and out of each wedge in turn in the manner shown by the lower needle.

CLOUD FILLING, figure 105.— The basis of this filling consists of a number of isolated stitches spaced regularly over the surface. To commence these, single stitches are either darned or by some other means placed in position. Then the surface thread is passed in zigzag fashion horizontally across the form to be covered in and out of the pre-

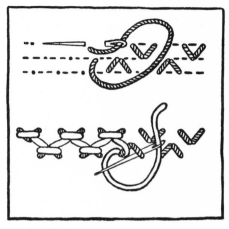

FIG. 104. RAISED CHEVRON STITCH.

liminarily laid foundation. Much of the effect depends upon the right setting out of the foundation stitches; these must be regularly and firmly laid down, their distance apart depending upon the thickness of the working threads, and upon what special effect may happen to be required.

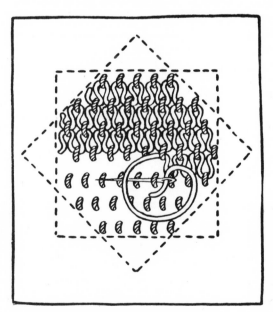

FIG. 105. CLOUD FILLING.

MALTESE CROSS FILLING, figure 106.—A geometrical filling is illustrated in the diagram. It is worked upon a foundation of interwoven threads, spaced at different intervals alternately nearer together and farther apart. When laying down the foundation it is necessary to interlace the threads because the surface stitching could not be worked out upon any other arrangement. In the diagram a partly worked element explains the method of execution. The working thread is brought to the surface just underneath one of the foundation threads (see arrow). After coming up through the ground fabric, it proceeds to wind in and out, round the corners of the square it is to fill, until the figure is complete. Its progress can be followed unfinished in the lower cross. The ground fabric is only entered at the start and finish of a unit. The elements need not necessarily be worked as closely together as seen here. For use upon a larger surface, leaving the alternate crosses out would perhaps make a better design, for the interlacing foundation threads would sufficiently decorate the empty spaces which occur between.

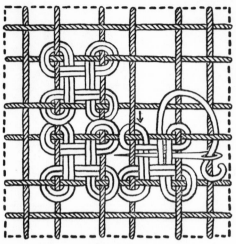

FIG. 106. MALTESE CROSS FILLING.

CRETAN OPEN FILLING, figure 107.—A bold and effective filling for a leaf is illustrated in the diagram. This is composed of a chequering of Cretan stitch worked upon previously laid lines of thread. Firm lines of thread are first laid at regular intervals across the leaf and Cretan stitch, explained on page 32, worked upon them, diagonally downwards, from right to left. In the diagram the fourth row of stitching is being put in and, where the needle is at work, the method of passing from one cluster to the next, besides the working of the first two stitches, can be followed. Sometimes a Bullion Knot of different colour is added in the spaces between. (See Plate XVII.)

RAISED HONEYCOMB FILLING, figure 108.—This filling makes an excellent flower centre for some types of work. Its effect, gained by raised stitching, is one of strong light and shade. Honeycomb Filling is worked upon a foundation of crossing threads. In the diagram, for the sake of clearness, these are shaded. This foundation consists of parallel lines crossed by similar ones at right angles. After laying these down, the next process is to overcast them. This overcasting is worked detached from the ground fabric, commencing with the underneath ones first. In the lower left-hand corner of the diagram the overcasting has been started. When the foundation threads in both directions are covered

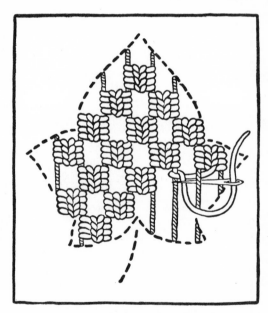

FIG. 107. CRETAN OPEN FILLING.

in this way, the needle proceeds to pass threads spirally round each line in turn, commencing in the manner shown in the third upright in the diagram. This thread only passes round the foundation thread, it does not enter the material but at start and finish. When the line, threading round one bar, is complete, it is then overcast with thread in just the same manner as the foundation threads were treated. Next, a line of thread is twisted round and round the same line again but in a contrary direction. This is illustrated upon the adjoining bar. It is then overcast, like the previous one. When all the upright threads are covered, the horizontal ones are next treated in similar fashion. The first half show little but serve as a kind of padding underneath the others.

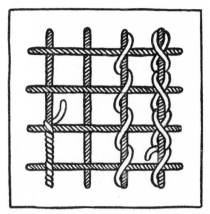

FIG. 108. RAISED HONEYCOMB FILLING.

DETACHED OVERCAST STITCH, figure 109.—This useful stitch can often be used in place of the better known Overcast, for it is perhaps the prettier form of the two. The difference between them is that this one is not stitched into the ground material; instead, it is worked upon a foundation of loosely worked Stem stitch. This gives it a detached, freer look which is difficult to describe, but of pleasing effect. The Stem stitch foundation must be worked so that it lies loosely upon the surface and only picks up the ground fabric at long intervals. A single line of this stitching can be seen in the working diagram, where it runs up the centre in an S form. It is not practical to overcast only upon a single Stem stitch line, either two or three are laid down as a rule. A second Stem stitching, shaded to distinguish it from the first, can be seen on the left in the diagram. It should be noted that it crosses

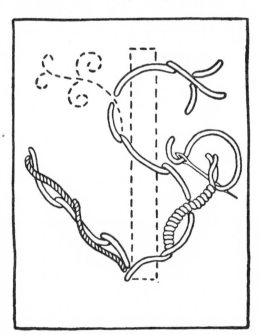

FIG. 109. DETACHED OVERCAST STITCH.

over the first line and picks up the ground fabric at a different point from it. There is little difficulty with the overcasting. It is worked in the same way as the ordinary variety excepting that it does not enter the ground fabric. The right effect is not obtained unless an absolutely even line of stitching results. To obtain this, the stitches must be laid close together, and always pick up the same number of foundation threads. One advantage of working Overcast in this manner is that it is easily possible to pass the stitch over or under a raised bar or other obstacle. For instance, a tendril, for which it is a particularly suitable stitch, may need to cross over a thick stem such as that suggested by the dotted band in the diagram. The Samplers in Plates VI and XVII both show this stitch in use.

SHEAF STITCH, figure 110.—This is a handsome border stitch. It works the circular band in Plate XI, and the stem in Plate XXA.

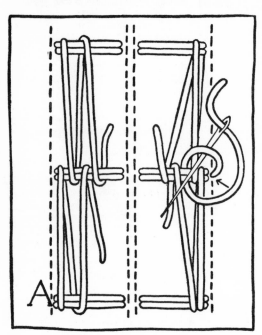

FIG. 110. SHEAF STITCH.

As with many stitches, the thread which works it out is an important factor in gaining the desired effect: a firm glazed one is a good variety to use. There are two different ways of working Sheaf. The one makes a narrower band and contains a lesser number of threads, whilst the other makes a broader and more important band of stitching. The method of working the broader band will be described first. Figure 110 explains the various processes in the execution. First put in some foundation stitches. These are laid across the band in pairs at regular intervals. The stitch is worked upon these transverse threads which should be of the same substance and kind as that used for the rest of the work. The working thread must now be brought through at point A in the figure. It should emerge at the outer edge of the first pair of cross threads. The first stage, that of passing it round two sets of the foundation threads, can best be followed by studying the drawing. If the working thread is fairly coarse, the band will be filled up when it has been passed to and fro about seven times. The same winding-round process is now repeated over the second and third set of transverse threads. This second set of laid stitches must be made to interlock with the first in the manner shown in the diagram. This second winding to and fro of thread is carried on continuously from the last one with the same needleful, and is taken in the opposite direction across the band—that is, from right to left. Then the third winding, over the next set of foundation threads, will naturally work in the same direction as the first. When this weaving to and fro of thread is completed as far as the band has to extend, the final stage of the execution must be commenced. This is illustrated in the figure where the needle is at work. It consists of a knotted line of stitching taken across from side to side of the band at the point where the threads interlock with each other. This knotted line is worked upon the transverse foundation threads. To carry it out, bring the thread through at the right side (see arrow in diagram). Slip the needle under the foundation threads, just beyond the first two surface threads, and then, when the thread is almost pulled through, pass the needle under the working thread and draw up tightly. This is in process in the diagram. The same proceeding is repeated just beyond the second pair of surface threads, and so on until the other side is reached.

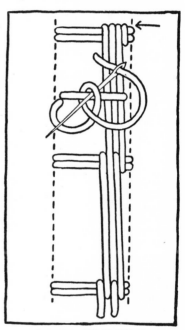

FIG. III. SHEAF STITCH (SIMPLER FORM).

This final knotting besides being ornamental has the effect of fixing the surface longitudinal threads securely in place, and of spreading them out in regular order across the width of the band. On looking at the worked example, in Plate XI, where the circular band is in Sheaf stitch, it will be seen that the long lines of thread first spread out to the entire width of the band, and are next sheathed together into a slightly narrower space. This gathering up is contrived by working a couple of Satin stitches with the needle midway between two of the knotted lines and it is done whilst passing from one completed knotted line to begin the next. With this variety of Sheaf stitch only half the sheaf of stitches shows upon the surface.

SHEAF STITCH (SIMPLER FORM), figure 111.—With the simpler Sheaf stitch the thread encircles the foundation threads once, and then passes on immediately to the next pair of threads, and so on to the end of the band. This completed, a second line is worked in the same manner and as many more as are necessary to fill in the width of the band. Then the knotted stitch, previously described, is worked across. In figure 111 an alternative form for the tying-in thread can be seen. Instead of the two Satin stitches, a single one is placed across first, and then a knot worked upon it for the second. After the needle has made the knot, it passes the thread to the back on the opposite side from which it started. Contrasting colours may be used, if wished, for the knotted line, and the tying-in stitches. The arrow points to the start of the first longitudinal thread. It commences by passing over and under the cross threads and then over again and on to the next pair below.

RAISED STEM STITCH BAND, figure 112.—Here Stem stitch is worked upon a previously laid foundation. The underlay consists, first, of a number of threads laid lengthwise along the band, arranged so as to be more raised in the centre than at the edges. Across these at fairly close regular intervals single stitches are laid at right angles to the padding thread. The next proceeding is to cover the surface with close lines of Stem stitch. This is commenced at the base and worked upwards, the stitch being entirely executed upon the transverse threads. Each line of Stem stitch may, at apex and base, emerge from the same hole in the centre of the band. This makes the lines of stitching converge together at these points and it gives a pleasant finish to the band. This treatment can be seen in Plate XVII, but not in this diagram. The needle shows the third row of Stem stitching in process of being worked. None of these rows is complete. They have been left unfinished to show the underlay. The lines of stitching must be pressed close to each other. Sometimes, as a finish, a transverse thread is laid across at top and base and covered with Overcast or Buttonhole stitch. (See Plate XVII.) This method of work can be used to fill other forms besides bands. For instance, with the right type of design it is pretty worked solidly over a leaf or flower. For this, the outline of the form should

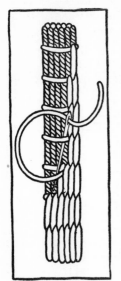

FIG. 112. RAISED STEM STITCH BAND.

not be too much indented, also there should be sufficient surface space to show the stitch to advantage.

CHEQUERED CHAIN BAND, figure 113.—This figure illustrates an ingenious stitch, contrived by working with two needles, and doubled, contrasted thread. If a raised effect is wanted, a padding of threads must be first laid down along the band and the transverse stitches seen in the diagram placed on top. The latter should be about one-sixteenth of an inch apart, for the effect is better when they are close. Thread two blunt-pointed needles with threads of contrasted colour. It is easier to work with one thread doubled in the needle rather than with two threaded in. To

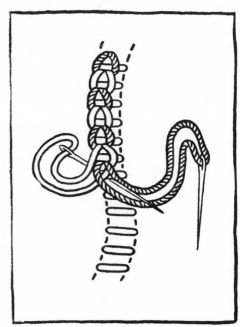

FIG. 113. CHEQUERED CHAIN BAND.

copy the diagram, commence by bringing the darker thread through at the apex. Pass it over the first bar and under the second, and then let it lie upon the material towards the right side as it is doing in the diagram. Now bring the needle with the lighter thread through to the surface just below the first bar, and as it is pulled through, make it at the same time pass between the two threads of the stitch just executed (see needle in diagram). Then let this lighter thread lie on the material for a moment, as the other one did, whilst the darker one is passed up through it, just below the second bar, in the same fashion. Then lay the darker one down and pick up the needle with lighter thread and so on; for this process is repeated again and again, taking up each needle in turn, until the end of the line is reached. Then a second line of Chequered Chain is started at the top and worked close beside the first. This continues until sufficient rows are worked to cover the foundation. If the second row is commenced with the light thread instead of the dark one, a chequered instead of a banded effect will be obtained, and it is just as effective. Both

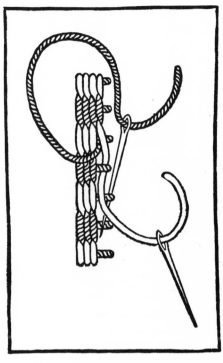

FIG. 114. STRIPED WOVEN BAND.

forms of this stitch can be seen in Plate VI.

STRIPED WOVEN BAND, figure 114.—If a raised effect is required for this stitch, begin by laying down some lines of thread along the band to pad it. Then across the padding lay a series of threads spaced about a sixteenth of an inch apart. Thread two needles, one with blue and the other with white thread, and bring both through the material just above the uppermost crossing thread at the left-hand end of it. The blue thread should be the

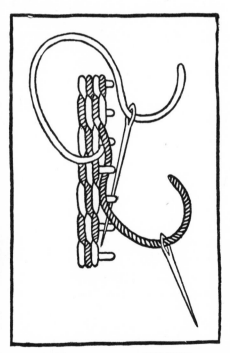

FIG. 115. DIAGONAL WOVEN BAND.

one most to the left. Pass the blue thread underneath the first bar and then let it lie upon the material. Pass the white thread over the first and under the second bar, drawing it through under the blue one now lying upon the material. Having passed under the blue thread, the white thread now rests upon the material. Take up the needle with blue thread, pass it over the second bar, under the third and also under the white thread, and then let it lie on the material. The needle in the diagram is carrying out the stage just described. This process is repeated, picking up each colour in turn, till the end of the band is reached. The threads are then started again at the top in exactly the same manner as before, always taking the white thread over the odd numbered bars, the first, third, fifth, and so on, and the blue one over the even numbered ones.

DIAGONAL WOVEN BAND, figure 115.—This variation needs but little explanation if the worker has executed the previously described Striped Band, for the working of the two is almost alike. Commence by first laying the padding threads and then throw the bars across them. Then bring the two threads through at the apex as before and work the first line down the bars in the same fashion. Instead of commencing the second row in the same manner, change the order of the coloured threads. In place of passing the blue thread under the first bar, pass the white one under, but the blue one over it and under the second, and so on. For the third row revert to the order of the first, and for the fourth to the order of the second. These stitches are as easily worked across a wider surface, such as a leaf, as across a band. In Plate XVII the leaves are filled in chiefly with this kind of stitch.

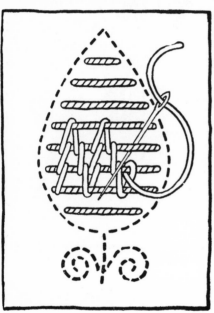

FIG. 116. CHEVRON-STEM STITCH.

CHEVRON-STEM STITCH, figure 116.—To understand this stitch, first glance at the completed leaf at the base of Plate XXXIII, and then at this diagram. In the sampler the effect of the completed filling, and, to a certain extent, the stitches, can be seen, whilst in the diagram the method of execution is shown. To commence, lines of stout thread must be laid horizontally across the leaf about one-eighth of an inch apart ; the exact spacing of these lines depends upon the size of the leaf and the coarseness of the working thread. To carry out this stitch perfectly the help of a frame is required. When the foundation of horizontal threads is completed, bring the working thread through on the left margin of the leaf just below one of the horizontal lines. Perhaps it is easiest to commence in the centre as shown in the diagram. The Stem stitch is now worked in a sloping direction upwards upon four horizontal lines in succession. It then passes down the same four in the manner illustrated. This zigzag movement is continued until the other side of the leaf is reached.

There the needle is passed through the material to the back (for the first time since the start) and is brought through to the front, underneath this point, immediately below the lowest horizontal line in the diagram. A similar line of zigzag Stem stitching is now worked from right to left, close to the one above, until it arrives at the starting-point again. In whichever direction the stitch is being worked it must always keep the thread on the same side, on the right of the needle, so that all the stitches are alike in appearance. This process is continued until the base of the leaf is filled in solidly with stitching. Then for completing the upper part commence working again, close by the first starting-point, and work gradually upwards till all is filled closely in.

Each fresh row of stitching starts from a margin and finishes in the opposite margin and the needle does not pierce the ground fabric on its journey across. The rows should be packed closely together and are most effective if carried out in two well-contrasted colours, for by this means the chevron form taken by the stitching is shown to advantage. (See Plate XXA.)

STEP STITCH, figure 117.—A decorative band of stitching suitable for use in a formal design is made by this variety. It is executed upon a preliminary laid foundation of parallel threads. To begin, work two perpendicular lines of Chain about half an inch apart. Then throw lines of thread horizontally across at regular intervals stretching from one Chain line to the other. The lines should be about one-eighth of an inch apart. The foundation complete, the thread is then brought to the surface just below the uppermost horizontal line at the left-hand side.

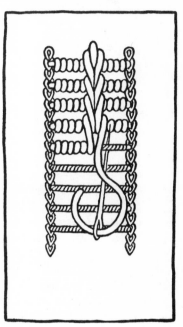

FIG. 117. STEP STITCH.

Now let the thread encircle this transverse line five times. This will have brought it near to the centre. As it passes across the surface of the bar for the sixth time, instead of taking it round as before, carry it a little higher up and pass it through to the back of the material about one-eighth of an inch above the bar. Bring the thread to the surface again, below the bar, in correct position for continuing the Overcast stitches, five more of which will complete the row. The second row is now worked in similar fashion to the first, excepting that when reaching the centre, the needle passes the thread round the long single stitch, in the manner seen in the diagram, thus forming a kind of Chain loop. Except at start and finish of a line the needle should not enter the ground fabric. Coarse twisted thread is the most effective kind to use, and the Chain lines at each side might be worked in a contrasting colour.

RAISED CHAIN BAND, figure 118.—Another simple surface stitch, worked upon a foundation of transverse threads, is represented here.

After preparing the foundation, the needle is brought through at the top, just above the first transverse thread. There it passes the thread once round the bar at the centre, and comes up again above it, on the left. Next a looped stitch is executed, similar to that the needle is working in the diagram. The stitch thus completed is worked successively over each bar in turn. Sometimes three Chain lines, instead of the one here seen, are worked down the band, and the one on each side of the central one can be of different colour. A band of this stitch worked in two colours can be seen on the margin of the Sampler in Plate XIII.

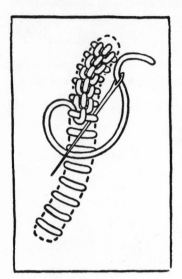

FIG. 118. RAISED CHAIN BAND.

PORTUGUESE BORDER STITCH, figure 119. — This surface stitch is often employed for stems or marginal lines. A preliminary foundation of transverse stitches must first be laid between the traced lines. This completed, the thread is brought through from the back below the lowest bar at its right-hand end. Then four stitches are worked round this and the next bar together, the thread, during the process, not entering the ground material. These completed, the needle must next be brought up in correct position for starting the second stitch ; this is just below the second bar and to the left of the last completed stitch. Two similar stitches are now worked over the second and third bars together, and then the thread must be brought up in position to work the next two stitches. This process is continued till the apex of the band is reached, and the same process is then carried through on the other side. This

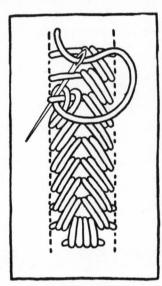

FIG. 119. PORTUGUESE BORDER STITCH.

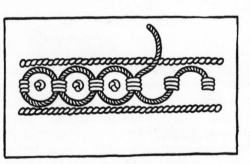

FIG. 120. GUILLOCHE STITCH.

is most easily worked if the position of the fabric is reversed. This stitch, with a Chain line added down the centre, can be seen on the margin of the worked sampler in Plate XVII.

GUILLOCHE STITCH, figure 120.—Two colours are employed to

work this border line. To carry out the margins either Chain or Stem stitch might be used. Next, in the centre between the two rows of stitching, work successive groups of three Satin stitches. These stitches might be contrived by means of three close lines of darning running from end to end of the band. The next proceeding is to pass a line of thread along, in and out of the central groups of stitches in the manner seen at the right-hand end of the diagram. When reaching the end of the band the

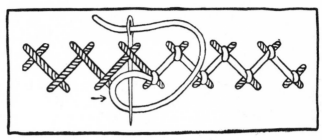

FIG. 121. TIED HERRINGBONE STITCH.

thread returns and again passes in and out of the central stitches, but in the opposite direction. A French or a Bullion knot is often placed in the centre of each circle to complete the band.

TIED HERRINGBONE STITCH, figure 121.—To those who are familiar with plain needlework Herringbone, and with Coral stitch, this variety needs little explanation, for it consists of a

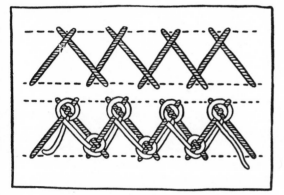

FIG. 122. LACED HERRINGBONE STITCH.

Coral knot worked upon a Herringbone line. The foundation of Herringbone must first be executed. This completed, a line of Zigzag Coral stitch is then worked upon it in the direction from right to left. Each Coral knot is fastened upon the Herringbone basis at the point where the threads cross. A stitch can be seen in process of formation in the diagram where the needle is at work.

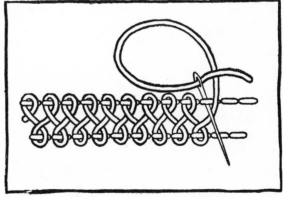

FIG. 123. INTERLACED BAND STITCH.

At the point marked by the arrow the left thumb holds down the working thread whilst the knot is being formed.

LACED HERRINGBONE STITCH, figure 122.—For this, a surface thread is wound in circular fashion twice round the foundation of

Herringbone at the crossing points of the stitches. Worked in two contrasting colours, it makes a decorative border stitch. The thread, whilst being wound round, must go alternately over and under the crossing foundation stitch, in the manner shown in the diagram. To make a more important line let the Herringbone basis cross more over itself and wind the surface thread several times round.

INTERLACED BAND STITCH, figure 123.—A stitch of this nature is useful for designs of mixed floral and geometrical type. It would carry out for example a diamond-shaped trellis over a surface, for it suits any kind of formal band design. The foundation, formed of a double line of Back stitch, is first worked. The stitches of the two lines are not placed exactly opposite each other, but

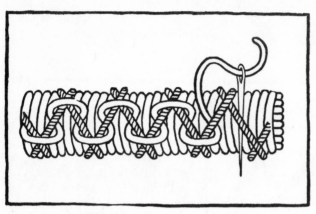

FIG. 124. RAISED LATTICE BAND.

alternately, as seen in the diagram. The next process is to interlace the surface thread to and fro between the double line of Back stitching.

RAISED LATTICE BAND, figure 124.—The raised appearance of this stitch is obtained by first laying down a padding of threads and then working a combination of several stitches upon it. Lay along the length of the band about half a dozen threads, letting them lie thicker at the centre than at the edges. A close line of Satin stitch covers this padding. On top of this a line of Herringbone stitch is placed. This passes to and fro across the raised band and enters the material on each side alternately. Finally the needle passes a thread in and out of the Herringbone band in the manner shown in the diagram.

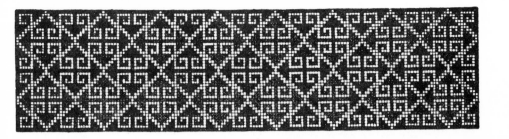

CHAPTER VII—CANVAS STITCHES

CANVAS embroidery was practised in England during the middle ages, for it occurs on existing vestments of that period. On the thirteenth-century English orphrey, preserved at Lyons, the foliage is entirely carried out in Tent stitch. The same stitch occurs upon some details on the magnificent cope preserved at Pienza. Again, on an English orphrey in the cathedral of Lerida in the north of Spain, there is an example of the use of Chequer stitch (figure 145) upon the lining of the mantle of one of the figures. A few centuries later canvas work was probably the most universal form of embroidery practised in the home, for by the middle of the seventeenth century, samplers, chiefly composed of it, had reached to a high level of perfection, also there were numerous pattern books in common use with most of their embroidery designs prepared for canvas work. The fine pictorial subjects, worked by this method, equal in their way to tapestry hangings, belong to this and the previous century, and there are the dainty little handbags and pincushions worked about this time with silks and metal threads in Gobelin, Tent, and Cross stitch.

Canvas work owes its peculiar character to the fact that the stitches base themselves upon the counted threads of the ground fabric. This gives a certain pleasing formality of treatment to every portion of the design. It is difficult in this branch of embroidery to copy a flower and make it naturalistic, some detail is perforce omitted, for it is hardly possible by this method of work to put it in. With some forms of needlework it is possible to imitate Nature almost to the extent of pretending to be the actual object. But such deception is hardly desirable, it is not advisable with needlework to try to imitate Nature exactly, or anything else ; what is required is an embroidery representation of the subject, and the more the needle and thread, with their accompanying convention of stitch, are in evidence the better.

With all canvas work it is especially important that the technique should be perfect, for to look well the stitches must be exactly similar in every detail. For either fine, close work or that of any size, it is necessary to work in a frame, but lighter work is easily done in the hand. In order to make the stitches absolutely regular and like each other, the portion which lies upon the reverse side of the material should be regular and alike, though not necessarily like the front. It is not possible, with an intricate pattern, to keep absolutely to this rule, but the idea should be kept in mind and carried out as far as possible.

CROSS STITCH, figure 125.—This, the best known of the canvas group, is a development of Tent stitch. It can be used for either fine

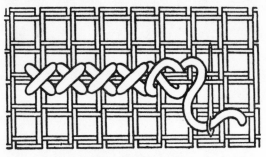

FIG. 125. CROSS STITCH.

or coarse work, and double thread canvas, which is illustrated in the diagram, is usually chosen for the ground. Cross stitch can be worked in different ways according to the purpose for which it is intended. For instance, when used for the marking of linen, initials and so forth, it is best worked either so that the stitching forms a neat square at the back or so that it is identical on both sides. The latter way is the more difficult to manipulate, but in both cases it is simply a question of ingeniously bringing the needle through at the right point. For filling in a solid ground, sometimes the first half of the stitch is worked entirely along a line and the crossing over done upon a return journey. This, though a quicker way, is not quite so good in effect as when each stitch is completed before another is started. In whatever manner the stitch is executed it is necessary always to work the final crossing

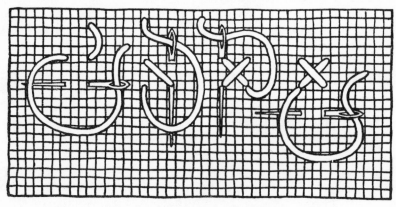

FIG. 126. MARKING CROSS STITCH

over in the same direction. The diagram shows the correct way to work Cross stitch. A loosened stitch at the end of the line explains the whole process. To commence the next stitch the thread is brought through as shown by the loose thread and the needle in the diagram. Should single thread canvas be preferred for use, the execution is practically the same, for the working thread usually passes over the same number of opposing ground threads, only there is more space between them. Cross stitch, when required on a much larger scale, can be worked over double the ordinary number of threads. Sometimes both the coarse and the fine

FIG. 127. ENLARGED DETAILS FROM THE COLOURED FRONTISPIECE.

H

stitch are used in the same piece of work. Loosely woven linen is often used for the ground instead of canvas. In cases where the background is not worked, linen is a necessity, and if hand-made, adds much to the beauty of the work. The stitch when executed on such material is sometimes taken across just one thread only of the fabric in each direction. The flowers in the Frontispiece are worked thus. (See also figure 127.) MARKING CROSS STITCH, figure 126.—For marking linen, and other purposes, it is useful to be able to work Cross stitch so that upon the back a neat square is built up. On the old samplers the signatures and dates are often worked in this stitch, sometimes with the square side uppermost and the cross underneath. In the diagram the way to execute the stitch with the cross on the surface is illustrated. To obtain the two-sided effect required, it is necessary to double one of the crossing stitches. This is seen in progress in the third stage of the working. The fourth illustrates the commencement of the second stitch. In the first stage the end of the thread can be seen left unfastened; on actual work this must be neatly secured at a point where an after stitch will cover it, for the aim with this form of Cross is to be perfect on both sides. Occasionally, when marking initials it is necessary to recross still further some of the already worked stitches in order to reach the point for continuation, though forethought may make this unnecessary.

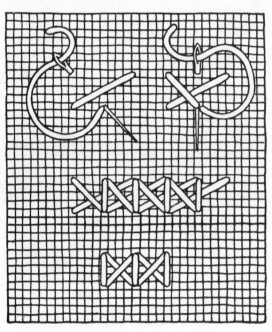

FIG. 128. MONTENEGRIN CROSS STITCH.

MONTENEGRIN CROSS STITCH, figure 128.—This, a pretty and quickly worked form of Cross stitch, is not as well known as it should be. Though different on the two sides of the ground fabric, it is effective on each, and so can be used when both sides may be exposed to view. The stitches are long and cover the ground quickly. The diagram explains the method of work, the lowest figure shows the appearance on the wrong side, the middle one the effect of the completed stitch on the right side, and the top two the way to execute it. Bring the needle to the surface, then pass it back after crossing over four horizontal and eight vertical threads of the ground fabric. Bring the thread to the surface again in the centre, below, as seen in the left-hand figure, where the needle is in process of working the next stage of the stitch which is a short one crossing the long one. The third stage, an upright stitch, can

*PLATE XVII*A. *DETAIL FROM EMBROIDERED SCREEN. Stitches used for the working—Diagonal Woven Band, Interlacing Wave Filling, Pekinese, Chained Border Faggot, Holbein.*

PLATE XVIII. THE QUARREL. *In Cross stitch in coloured silks on hand-made linen. The discs forming part of the fringe are in Spiral Trellis. (Half full size.)*

be seen in process to the right. This is an excellent variety for filling a solid background.

LONG-ARMED CROSS STITCH, figure 129.—This differs from ordinary Cross in that one of the crossing stitches is of double length. This innovation enables it to cover the ground more rapidly and avoids the square appearance of the better known stitch. It is quicker in the working than Montenegrin and more economical, for there is less thread at the back. The method of work is shown in the diagram where the uppermost figure explains the execution. Below this three completed stitches can be seen, and at the base, the appearance of these three stitches on the other side of the fabric. Long-armed Cross is a quick and effective ground stitch. The thickness of thread used in the working decides whether the ground fabric will be completely covered up or just allowed to show through in places. Either way is permissible, the former the most usual. (See margin of Plate I.)

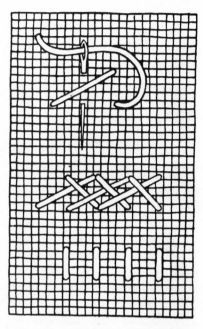

FIG. 129. LONG-ARMED CROSS STITCH.

TWO-SIDED ITALIAN CROSS STITCH, figures 130, 131.—This stitch, alike on both sides, can be worked either upon loosely woven linen or upon canvas. The Italian workers of the sixteenth century used this stitch a great deal and executed it upon loosely woven handmade linen. The stitch consists of a cross with single stitches enclosing it upon the four sides. These can be clearly seen in figure 131. A characteristic, not visible there, is that the various stitches which build it up are always drawn through tightly whilst the work is in progress. This draws together the threads of the ground fabric which results in tiny perforations being formed between all the stitches. There is a certain relative proportion neces-

FIG. 130. TWO-SIDED ITALIAN CROSS STITCH.

sary between the size of working thread and ground fabric which can only be discovered by trial. If the thread is too coarse for the ground, the perforation will be practically filled up and the effect lost, whilst if it is too fine the stitches will not serve to cover completely the threads of ground material. Either of these conditions mars the effect of the stitch. It is well to use a blunt-pointed needle, some sizes larger than

H 2

necessary. The use of this prevents any splitting of fabric threads and serves to emphasise the perforations. Usually, with two-sided Italian Cross, the method of working the ground and leaving the pattern in the plain linen is adopted. Figure 130 shows the four stages of working.

The stitches usually pass over three threads of ground fabric. There is an alternative method of working which is sometimes more practical. Having completed the third stage (see figure 130), instead of putting in the final diagonal stitch, commence a fresh one and work in this incomplete fashion till reaching the end of the row. Then complete the crossing of each stitch in turn, in the manner shown by the needle in figure 131, until the left side is reached. This is the better way of the two to execute the stitch, for it is now exactly alike on both sides. It is usual to work in rows from

FIG. 131. TWO-SIDED ITALIAN CROSS STITCH (VARIATION).

the base upwards and a row is not really complete until the one above is worked, for this supplies the final top stitch of the square. Carrying out straight lines is a simple matter, but, at times, when executing a pattern, difficulties present themselves of having to pass from one point to another and of working isolated stitches. There should be as few of these as possible, and a designer who understands the technique will arrange for this, but still there must remain some few. This stitch can be worked equally well from the upper or under side of the material—so sometimes when at the end of a line and wishing to return, the simplest plan is to reverse the position of the material and come back working upon the under side. Besides this, there are the alternative ways of working already described, and if all these aids fail, the worker must travel to the necessary point by duplicating some of the stitches—that is, by passing a second time across or up the side of a square, on front or back, until the goal is reached.

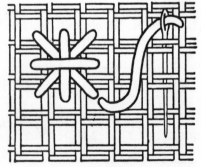

FIG. 132. DOUBLE-CROSS STITCH.

DOUBLE-CROSS STITCH, figure 132.—This stitch is effective and covers the ground quickly. An ordinary Cross stitch is worked first and then an upright Cross is placed upon it. The stitch can be used either for outline or for solidly filled patterns or grounds, and is best applied to bold types of work. When worked upon very coarse canvas, sometimes it is advisable to add four more stitches in order to cover the ground more completely. These four added stitches when correctly placed would join the four extremities of the upright cross. They should be worked before this upright cross is placed in position, because in order to preserve the character of the stitch this should come last. If the space between each stitch and the next is too large, a single long stitch can be laid regularly between to fill up the gaps, and the same treatment can occur at top and base. The groups of stitches need not necessarily occur exactly beneath each other, a half-stitch placed at the commencement of each line of the alternate rows will remove the squared-up appearance of the surface, which might for some purposes be too marked a feature.

HOLBEIN STITCH, figure 133.—
Holbein, known also as Line stitch, is a useful variety either for outline work or for using in conjunction with other canvas stitches. Combined with Cross it is particularly good. Holbein, when worked in a certain way, has the quality, sometimes a useful one, of being alike on both sides of the material. Figure 133 illustrates this way of working. The needle carries the thread by means of a regular, running stitch, all round the pattern. This process works just half the necessary stitching. The pattern is completed by the same running stitch being taken round again, in the contrary direction, this time picking

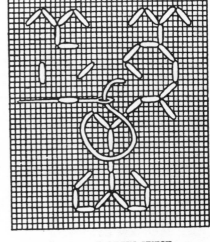

FIG. 133. HOLBEIN STITCH.

up the material so as to fill up the gaps left by the first running. In order to keep the stitching alike on both sides, forethought is sometimes necessary. If a single stitch branches off from the main pattern, the best way is to complete it on both sides of the fabric at the same time by means of a single Satin stitch. An example of this occurs in the diagram. The needle at work is just at the point where such a Satin stitch needs to be taken. (See completed portion exactly opposite.) Sometimes a group of stitches, running off at a tangent, have to be completed at the first working, and then the main part of the pattern continued in the ordinary way. A linen canvas, of regular mesh, forms the best ground fabric for working upon. Patterns

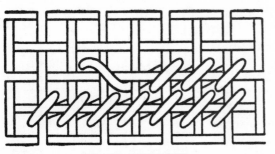

FIG. 134. TENT STITCH.

executed in this stitch occur several times in Holbein's pictures, hence its name. The alternative way of working the stitch is to treat it like Back stitch.

TENT STITCH, figure 134.—This is the finest of the canvas stitches, and perhaps the one in which the most beautiful work has been done. It is composed of a single small stitch taken across a warp and a woof thread of the ground fabric. The working diagram has been drawn in a manner which explains the working rather than in one which shows the right appearance of the stitch, for if drawn in the latter way, the stitches should completely cover up the canvas ground. It is important that the canvas should be hidden from sight; this is, however, only a question of

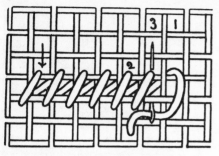

FIG. 135. GOBELIN STITCH.

suiting correctly the mesh of the canvas to the thickness of the working thread. Tent stitch is always worked on single thread canvas. Examination of the diagram will show that this stitch, when correctly worked, is longer on the reverse side than on the front. To commence, bring the needle and thread through at the left-hand end of the lower line of stitching and at the upper end of the first stitch. Take it through to the back, just below this point and a little to the left. The continued working, which is simply repetition, can be followed in the diagram all along the line. For the second row, which is most naturally executed in a contrary direction, the working is reversed, in order to keep the stitch alike at the back as well as at the front, for if it were not so treated, the surface would have a line-like appearance, which is especially to be avoided. To pass from the end of the first row to the beginning of the next, the thread is brought up as illustrated in figure 135. Sometimes Tent-stitch is worked over a previously laid thread. This raises it just a little, and ensures the complete covering up of the ground. To do this, a thread of like colour is stretched from end to end of the line to be worked and the stitch each time passed over it.

GOBELIN STITCH, figure 135.—This is one of the most useful canvas stitches, for either shaded work or backgrounds. The way to work Gobelin is illustrated in the diagram. It is not always possible to keep to this method. Sometimes the needle is forced to take a short upright stitch at the back like that in figure 137 instead of the slanting one seen in the diagram, but this has the effect of dividing the rows of stitches into distinctly marked lines. To work Gobelin, bring the thread through at the point marked by the arrow in the diagram, then take it downward over two horizontal and one perpendicular thread of the ground and pass it to the

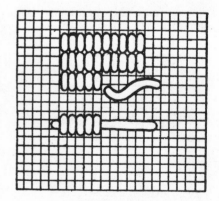

FIG. 136. UPRIGHT GOBELIN.

back. The remainder of the working can be followed in the figure. Upon reaching the end of a line the needle takes a short upright stitch (see diagram) to reach the point for commencing the next row which, if the work is continuous, has to come back in the contrary direction. To continue this row the needle takes the thread to the back at point 1, returns it to the front at point 2, then down at 3, and so on.

UPRIGHT GOBELIN, figure 136.—This variation is effective for some purposes. If, when working, the stitches do not entirely cover up the ground, a thread may be previously laid along underneath as shown in the lower portion of the diagram.

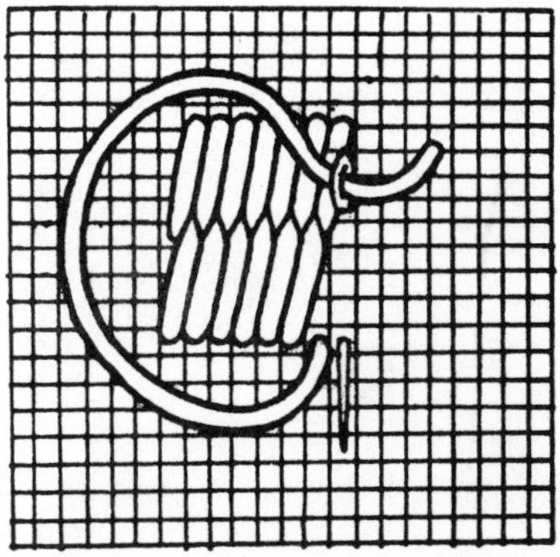

ENCROACHING GOBELIN STITCH, figure 137.—Another variation is to make each fresh row of slanting stitches slightly encroach upon the last worked row instead of just touching it. This variety of treatment can be applied to many embroidery stitches and it is excellent for shaded work. The stitch, it should be noted, is longer than the ordinary one, for it passes

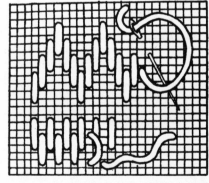

FIG. 137. ENCROACHING GOBELIN.

across five horizontal threads of the canvas ground. Gobelin Stitch, as the diagram shows, is usually worked upon single thread canvas. Double thread can be used, however, and another effective way of treating it is to allow each fresh row of stitches to encroach half-way up those of the first row—that is in practically the same way that Florentine stitch is illustrated in the lower portion of figure 139.

PLAITED GOBELIN STITCH, figure

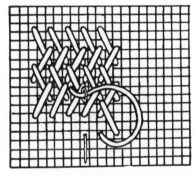

FIG. 138. PLAITED GOBELIN.

138.—This variety is a development of the Encroaching Gobelin Stitch, for it is the same stitch under different treatment. It is worked backwards and forwards and the direction of the slant of the stitches varies with the alternate rows. This variation in the stitch direction gives an interwoven effect to the surface, which is effective upon a background. (See Plate XXXIII.)

FLORENTINE STITCH, figure 139.—This stitch is suitable for the execution of geometrical patterns, especially those which can be carried

FIG. 139. FLORENTINE STITCH.

out by means of oblique lines, for Florentine is best worked in this direction rather than horizontally. It is a good stitch for heraldic work and also for floral designs when a strictly formal treatment is required. The working can be learned by a glance at figure 139. The upper of the two methods illustrated shows the usual and most straightforward method of working this stitch, whilst the lower figure shows how to proceed when it is necessary to work in horizontal lines. A quantity of canvas work in Florentine stitch has been done for chair seats, hangings, etc. It is mostly of geometrical design and of Italian origin, hence the name. The stitch usually passes over four horizontal threads of the canvas ground, though the number of threads may vary according to requirement. The number chosen must be an even one, for an odd number of threads would not work.

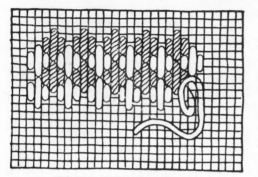

FIG. 140. HUNGARIAN STITCH.

HUNGARIAN STITCH, figure 140.—The stitch illustrated in the diagram is often seen in canvas embroidery, used for filling in a background whilst, perhaps, Tent or Cross stitch works out the intricacies of the pattern. The use of Hungarian upon the ground gives it a pretty satin-like effect. The stitch is worked in horizontal rows, the thread passing in vertical direction over first two, then four, and then two, horizontal threads of ground fabric. The diagram shows the manner in which each row fits into the

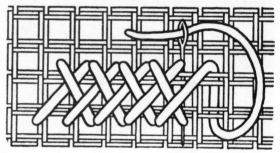

FIG. 141. PLAIT STITCH.

next. To make this clear, the rows are made up of different coloured threads, but in actual work the effect of one colour throughout is perhaps best. A simple variation on this stitch would be to make each diamond shape larger by letting it contain five instead of three stitches.

PLAIT STITCH, figure 141.—This is a quickly worked canvas stitch, useful for backgrounds. Sometimes the pattern is left plain with an outline round it, and then this stitch solidly covers the ground. The working can be followed in the diagram. When correctly done, the reverse side of the canvas should exhibit a neat row of short perpendicular lines, each composed of two single stitches. The needle, in order to effect the crossing of the threads, has to take a stitch alternately forward and backward.

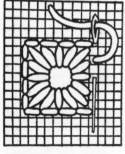

FIG. 142. EYE STITCH.

EYE STITCH, figure 142.—An attractive canvas stitch is illustrated in the diagram. It can be used to replace Cross for carrying out lettering, as so often seen on the old samplers. It carries out patterns based on chequers well, and it can be used, like other varieties of canvas stitches, for the fillings of large conventional flower or other forms. The most noticeable characteristic of this stitch lies in the perforation, which occurs in the centre. To emphasize this feature it is well to work in light colours, for these contrast well with the hole in the centre. To work Eye stitch, commence with the middle portion first. This is composed of sixteen stitches which are on their outer edges spread out round the four sides of a square. On their inner edges the stitches all pass through the same hole in the centre. These stitches, during the working, are pulled taut, to increase the size of the central perforation. When the sixteen stitches are worked, a row of Back stitches is placed round the margin of the square.

ALGERIAN EYE STITCH, figure 143.—Some lovely embroideries can be, and have in the past been, produced by the aid of this stitch, which is a simple form of the Eye stitch just explained. The completed stitch covers over a tiny square comprising four threads of ground fabric in each direction, and the surface is decorated by alternate squares of this size being either worked or left plain, which gives it a chequered effect. The stitch looks best when worked on a loosely woven fabric of light texture. Floss silk makes a good working thread, though any kind, not tightly twisted, can be used. Figure 143 illustrates four Eye stitches, the uppermost one being in process of execution. Each eyelet is composed of sixteen stitches. They are worked, like the spokes of a wheel, round a tiny square of the linen ground. The needle comes up always at the same point in the centre, works a couple of stitches first into the corner, then a couple in the centre of the side, having missed one interstice of the fabric threads, then a couple in the next corner, and so on till the square is complete. Each fresh square starts from the corner of the last one. The working thread must be pulled taut. It is usual to work a kind of stem round the outline of a pattern carried out in Algerian Eye, and sometimes small portions of it, centres of flowers and so forth, are filled in with a closer stitch such as Tent or Gobelin. If care is taken, the work can be practically alike on both sides. There are some beautiful examples worked in this stitch in the Victoria and Albert Museum, labelled 'Algerian, XVI century.' Some of these are curtains, and they are made of vertical bands of embroidered work joined together

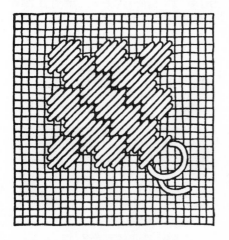

FIG. 144. DIAGONAL STITCH.

by striped silk ribbons : the effect of the whole is most original and pretty, for pattern, colour and materials used, are all well chosen.

DIAGONAL STITCH, figure 144.—The diagram illustrates a simple method of working a background in a diagonal chevron pattern. The stitch is carried from the upper left to the lower right side. The first stitch passes diagonally across two threads of fabric in each direction, then across three, then four, and gradually back to two again. If, where the stitches meet each other, the ground appears at all open, a Back stitch can be worked in zigzag direction to hide the junctions of the rows of stitching.

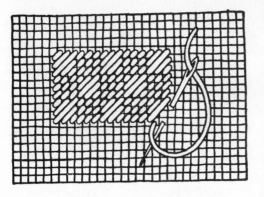

FIG. 145. CHEQUER STITCH.

CHEQUER STITCH, figure 145.—Alternating squares of like size filled respectively with long and with short stitches give a pleasant chequered appearance to a surface. Decorating a ground by a small geometrical pattern, such as this for example, instead of covering it monotonously with one stitch, is often a pretty treatment. Sometimes it is possible to adopt such a treatment, though at other times absolute monotony upon the ground is essential to show up the beauty of the pattern. The working is explained by the diagram. Each tiny square is composed of three threads of ground fabric in each direction. The first square is filled in with five large and the next with nine small stitches. The surface can be of one colour, for the two tones created by the change of stitch, make sufficient variation.

ROCOCO STITCH, figure 146.—This variety, though not much practised to-day, is often seen on work of the early sampler period. It is an adaptation of Roumanian to a canvas ground. The stitch is suitable for working small dainty objects, such as hand-bags, pincushions, needlecases, etc. Both ground and pattern are always completely covered by the stitching, and fairly light colours should be chosen for use, white being a particularly good background colour.

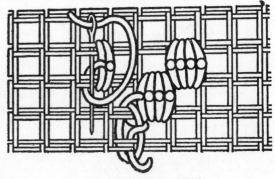

FIG. 146. ROCOCO STITCH.

Light colours should be chosen, because in a piece of work carried out in Rococo, there results, from the method of working, a regular perforation of tiny holes over the surface. These being dark show up best against a light ground, and they should show clearly, for it is these which give the work

PLATE XIX. 'OF GARDENS.' *In Cross stitch,*
in coloured silks on hand-made linen. (Half full size.)

PLATE XX. DRAWN FABRIC FILLINGS. *Outlines of leaves and scrolling stems in Overcast Chain. Marginal lines in Zigzag Chain.*

its character. When choosing or designing a pattern for execution in this stitch, it is necessary to adopt one which can be worked fairly straightforwardly in slanting lines, for this is the most direct method of carrying it out. Formal floral devices and geometrical patterns are well suited to its limitations. Double thread canvas of a special kind makes the best ground fabric. It should be pliable and have the horizontal threads stouter than the upright ones. To work the stitch, bring the thread through, and after passing it over four horizontal threads, take it to the back immediately below—that is, in the square next but one. This forms the long part of the stitch. Next a small crossing stitch ties the longer one down at the centre. To do this the thread is brought through in the adjoining square above to the right, and taken to the back immediately after crossing over the already formed stitch. During this tying down process, the thread also passes over two perpendicular threads of the canvas. Three more stitches are worked in the same way and then the thread is passed down to the correct point for commencing the filling of the next square. The way in which this is done is shown in the lower portion of the diagram, where the loosened stitches illustrate both the passing down and the working of the first stitch. Four stitches usually fill a square nicely, but more could be put if necessary. The thread should be pulled fairly tightly during the working, for this draws the threads of the fabric together and makes the perforations occurring between the stitches more visible. To obtain the right effect, it is necessary that there should be the correct proportion between the thickness of the working thread and the size of the mesh of the canvas ground, otherwise either the threads of the ground fabric will show, or the perforations will be closed up, owing to the employment of too thin or too thick a working thread.

CHAPTER VIII—DRAWN FABRIC STITCHES

THESE stitches are used chiefly in white embroidery. They gain their effect by drawing together in certain parts the threads of the fabric which results in the other parts being open or perforated. By this means all kinds of geometrical patterns can be built up which have a most refining effect upon a design. They are used either upon the background or on the ground of the pattern. Sometimes by the help of these stitches parts of the background can be made of different texture from the rest as in Plate XVI. These open ground stitches are effective when seen with the light behind as well as in the ordinary way.

Owing to the particular technique of this group it is especially important to choose suitable ground fabric. It should be of an even mesh, and somewhat loosely woven. If unsuitable stuff is used, the stitching may be correct yet ineffective in spite of much labour. The working thread should be fine and as like as possible to the background, for it needs to be little seen; the effect aimed at is not one of stitches, but of patterned fabric. In the diagrams explaining these stitches the drawing together of the fabric threads is not illustrated, they are only intended to show the correct stitching. Neatness is a quality of much value with this work; there should be no evidence upon the surface of a thread at the back passing from one row to the next—forethought often avoids even the necessity for this. A needle large in size and of blunt point is the kind to use, for its size helps to emphasise the perforations, and its bluntness avoids any splitting of the fabric threads. These stitches are easily invented, the variations here illustrated may suggest many others to an ingenious worker.

CHAINED BORDER STITCH, figure 147.—This can be worked tautly so as to draw the ground fabric together or be stitched just as is shown in the diagram. It can be worked either horizontally or obliquely across the fabric; both methods are illustrated. The ground fabric should be of an even mesh as the stitch is worked by counting its threads. The upper two of the four lines of stitching seen in the diagram are worked first and afterwards the lower two. To work the portion illustrated, commence by bringing the needle through at the point marked by the arrow. Turn the material the other way round, for the stitch is worked from left to right. Pass the working thread to the back

*PLATE XX*A.   *THE FLOWERING TREE.   Stem in Sheaf stitch,   Flowers in Interlacing.*
Leaves in Portugese Border.   Owls in Chevron Stem.   Bird's heads in Spiral Trellis.   Scroll work
in Double Knot.   Ground of centre panel in Single Faggot.   In the border occur Raised Stem
Band, Interlacing, Trellis, Fishbone, Faggot, and Overcast.

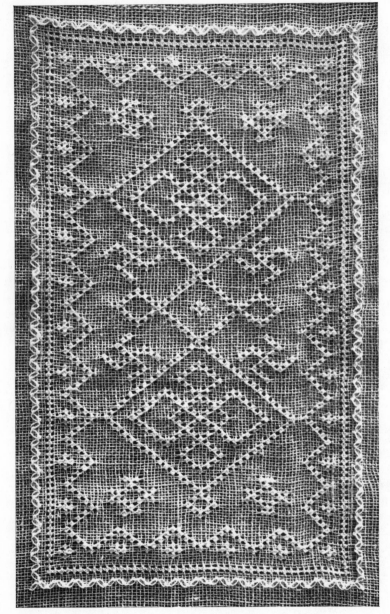

PLATE XXI. Geometrical Pattern in Indian Drawn Ground stitch.
Border in Knotted Cable Chain. Inner border in Four-sided stitch.

four threads farther along, and bring it to the surface on the line below two threads nearer the starting-point. The action of the needle at work in the diagram shows the entire execution, for it is simply a repetition of this, on one line or the other, each time. When the upper half of the band is complete, reverse the material so as to continue working from left to right. Though there are four rows of stitches, these cover only three threads of fabric. (See diagram.)

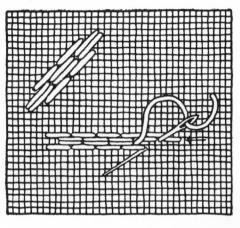

FIG. 147. CHAINED BORDER STITCH.

INDIAN DRAWN-GROUND STITCH, figure 148.—This stitch can be used to carry out an entire design. It is particularly effective when seen with the light behind it, as would be the case, for example, if used upon a window blind. It can only be executed in lines which run diagonally upon the mesh of the ground fabric, so in preparing a design for this stitch this is a necessary point to remember. A blunt-pointed needle should be used and a light and openly woven material makes the best working ground. (See Plate XXI.) In the diagram the crossing diagonal lines represent each thread of ground fabric, and two rows of the stitching are shown in progress. It is usual, though not necessary, to work the stitch thus in double lines backing upon each other. To work Indian Drawn-ground stitch, bring the working thread through at the perforation marked A, having previously fixed the end of the thread in the portion of fabric immediately above it. The needle proceeds to pass the thread in and out of the material in a succession of small, round loops, first over three threads, then under three, and again over and under three, thus reaching the starting-point. Then in order to reach the correct point for forming a second, similar loop, the needle passes over

FIG. 148. INDIAN DRAWN-GROUND STITCH.

the first three threads again and under three others more towards the left. It is now in position for carrying out a second circular loop. The process of passing from one loop to the next and of commencing a fresh one is in process in the diagram, where the needle is at work. When the

I

upper line is complete, the best plan is to reverse the position of the material and work a second line in the same way. The exact position of the two lines with regard to each other is important; the diagram clearly illustrates what this should be. Having mastered the stitch the worker will want to build up more imposing figures by its means. Developments based upon diagonal lines are easily planned when the limitations of the stitch are understood. Isolated elements can be introduced in a design. (See Plate XXI). For very delicate work, an openly woven soft mull muslin stitched with gossamer thread is dainty. Exquisite examples of this can be found on fine white Indian embroidery of fairly modern date. Close examination of some of this work revealed the fact that every fourth thread of the ground fabric had been withdrawn in both directions, thus saving the worker the trouble, when executing the stitch, of counting the threads which, on such fine fabric, would have been tedious.

THREE-SIDED STITCH, figure 149.—The diagram displays a geo-

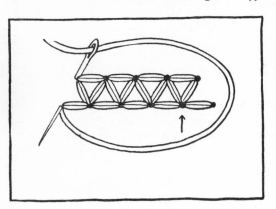

FIG. 149. THREE-SIDED STITCH.

metrical band composed of small like-sized Back stitches which are worked tightly in order to draw together the threads of the ground. Thus at the points where the stitches meet, small perforations appear in the fabric. Working with a larger needle than the size of thread demands helps to gain the required effect. The Back stitches are worked in the following order. To begin, the needle brings the thread to the surface at the point shown by the arrow. Then a couple of Back stitches are taken horizontally in succession over the same six threads of fabric. The needle is now at the starting-point. The next couple of Back stitches are taken, in a slanting direction inclining towards the right, over six threads of fabric in height and three in width. At the completion of the second of these stitches, the needle is brought up, not at the starting-point, but six stitches farther towards the left on the upper edge of the band. It is now in position for working the first couple of horizontal Back stitches in the upper row. Then, from the same point, two more are worked in a slanting direction downwards, leaning towards the right. At the completion of these two stitches, the needle is brought to the surface upon the lower edge of the band, six threads farther to the left than the starting-point. It now proceeds to go through the above-described process over again. This stitch could be treated as an all-over ground stitch by working row beneath row in succession, omitting the uppermost line in all but the top row.

FOUR-SIDED STITCH, figures 150, 151.—This neat line stitch is illustrated in figure 151 and in the upper part of figure 150. In the latter, in the top row, the three successive stages of a single stitch are shown and the dotted lines show the passage of the thread on the underside. The second row shows a band of the stitch partly worked, the needle here being in the act of passing to the point for executing the third stage of the fourth stitch. In the lower part of the diagram, the stitch is shown adapted to an oblique form of working. (See description of next variety.) In figure 151 the Four-sided stitch is shown drawing together the threads of the ground fabric. When treated as a drawn stitch like this it is usual to withdraw a thread of the warp both above and below the stitching as there seen.

FIG. 150. FOUR-SIDED STITCH AND SINGLE FAGGOT STITCH.

SINGLE FAGGOT STITCH, figure 150.—In the lower portion of figure 150 an adaptation of Four-sided stitch as an all-over filling is shown. This, known as Single Faggot, is worked obliquely and the square is executed in two journeys, the first works the upper two sides of the square and the second the lower two. The needle at work in the first line, and the loosened stitch and end of thread in the second line, together with the dotted lines showing the under thread, sufficiently explain the method of work. The constant drawing of the thread tightly must not be forgotten as this adds a pleasant feature to the stitch. This is a useful variety for working backgrounds or for pattern fillings. It can be seen in use in Plates XXA and XVI.

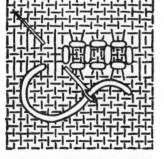

FIG. 151. FOUR-SIDED STITCH.

The working thread should be fine and like the fabric, for it should be almost invisible. Sometimes it is purposely of a deeper tint than the ground in order to lower its tone.

DOUBLE FAGGOT STITCH, figure 152.—This variety is a slightly more complex form of the oblique square stitch just described. It makes an effective ground stitch and looks well upon both upper and under side of the fabric. Seen against the light the effect is that of perforations constantly repeating over the ground divided by solid bars. Double Faggot stitch consists of a couple of stitches taken in succession over two threads of ground fabric, first horizontally and then vertically in alternation. The stitch is worked obliquely across the surface and the thread always pulled taut. In the diagram three lines of it are in process of execution. The central one, almost completed, runs from edge to edge of the square. In the other two rows, the different actions of the two needles show, first, how to work a couple of upright stitches and then how to pass obliquely along the under side to be in position for working two horizontal stitches.

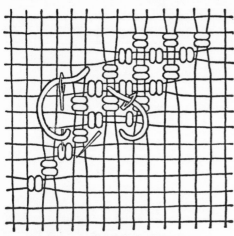

FIG. 152. DOUBLE FAGGOT STITCH.

SQUARED GROUND STITCH, figure 153.—This is in appearance like the upper stitch in figure 150, the difference between them lies chiefly in the execution. This is worked as an all-over filling, the other as a line stitch, and this difference makes a change in the method of work necessary. It is useful for lightly ornamenting backgrounds of embroideries. The stitch is worked most easily upon the under side of the fabric. The method of execution is shown in the upper portion of the diagram. In the lower portion is seen the effect upon the right side when three rows of the stitching have been completed. Having brought the thread through at the starting-point (see arrow) the needle carries it diagonally across the first little square, composed of four warp and four woof threads of ground fabric, passes it through to the back at the upper right-hand corner, and brings it to the front, four threads farther to the left, just as the needle is doing farther along. Next the needle passes to the back at the upper right-hand corner of the same square, and comes again to the surface immediately below, at the lower right-hand corner, and is now in position to repeat the process over again. The loosened stitch in the diagram represents the one which was worked immediately before the one in process with the needle. This is continued to the end of the line and then a second row is commenced at the left side immediately beneath the first. This second row can be worked in the other direction by reversing the position of the material. The first row is not complete

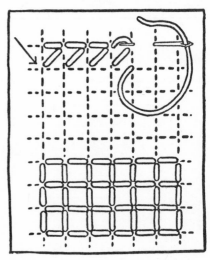

FIG. 153. SQUARED GROUND STITCH.

until the row below it is worked. For the first stitch of each row, and again when working entirely along the base, it is necessary to put in an extra stitch in order to complete the squares, otherwise two sides of the finished work would not have the outside edges of the squares completed.

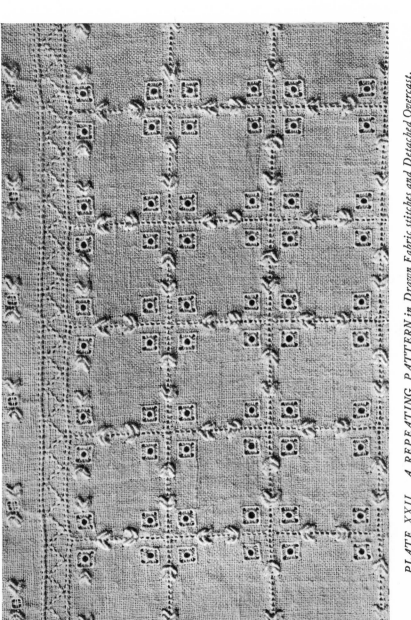

PLATE XXII.   A REPEATING PATTERN in Drawn Fabric stitches and Detached Overcast.

PLATE XXIII. SCENES FROM 'THE BLUE BIRD.' *The fillings in Drawn Fabric stitches, powderings and Pattern Drawing; in blue and white linen thread.*

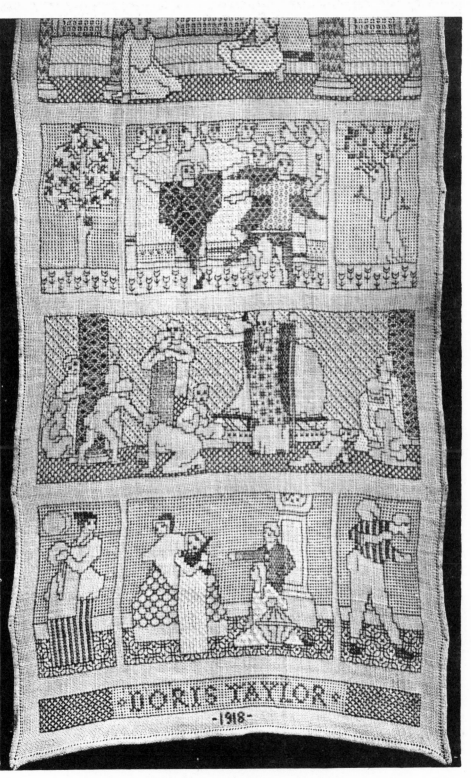

PLATE XXIV. *Lower part of Sampler XXIII.*

PLATE XXV. PATTERNS FOR BLACK WORK FILLINGS.

In black cotton upon fine single thread canvas.

These are put in whilst the work goes on and they take the form of a single Satin stitch, alike on both sides of the fabric. A subsidiary ground pattern, such as this, is worked before the superficial embroidery pattern is carried out. A large, blunt-pointed needle should be used and the thread must be pulled tautly. It is most perfectly worked in a frame. The number of threads of the ground fabric over which the stitch is worked can vary. Three or four are most usual.

FIG. 154. DIAGONAL RAISED BAND.

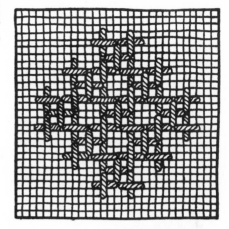

FIG. 155. OPEN TRELLIS FILLING.

DIAGONAL RAISED BAND, figure 154.—This stitch builds up a series of narrow, slightly raised bands across the material, and the plain ground between is usually filled in with the Single Faggot stitch. In Plate XX the two are used thus together. To execute it, bring the thread through at the point marked by an arrow. The upper needle shows the working of the first stitch. Upon reaching the end of the line a return journey is made down the same route (see lower needle). Each time a stitch is taken, pull the working thread taut, for this draws up the fabric and thus raises the band. When the one raised band is complete, proceed to work as many rows of Single Faggot stitch (figure 150) as are necessary to cover the space before the next raised band is required.

OPEN TRELLIS FILLING, figure 155.—When Diagonal Raised Band is imposed upon itself and worked in two directions it forms a pretty open trellis over the surface. It is worked thus upon a leaf in the lower part of Plate XX. Single Faggot stitch is not used with it here and the raised bands must

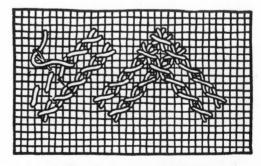

FIG. 156. CHEQUER FILLING.

be spaced at exactly the right distance apart to gain this particular effect. Figure 156 illustrates the same treatment, but the working is over a different number of fabric threads.

CHEQUER FILLING, figure 156.—Still another arrangement of a

diagonal band imposed upon itself is explained by the diagram. In Plate XX this stitch occurs upon a berry and on the frontispiece upon the arches. It is quite different in appearance from the last one though worked in similar fashion, and it shows what different results may be obtained by the simple means of varying the number of fabric threads worked over, and the distance apart of the lines of stitching. With this knowledge an ingenious worker will easily devise many new patterns. DIAGONAL CHEVRON, figures 157, 158.—This variety makes a waved diagonal line. It is usual to work it in bands with Single Faggot stitch between.

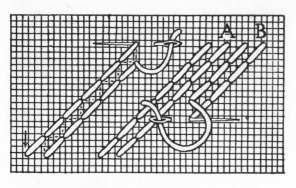

FIG. 157. DIAGONAL CHEVRON.

It can be used without any surrounding stitching, for by itself it makes a decorative line. For example, it might be applied to such a purpose as the dividing up of a surface into diamond shapes by means of crossing lines. In figure 157 two stages of the stitch are illustrated and figure 158 shows the final stage. The first two stages are worked upon the reverse side of the material, the third upon the right side. To work the first, bring through the thread at the point marked by an arrow in the diagram. Insert the needle after passing it diagonally across a square composed of three threads and bring it out three threads below. Take a second similar diagonal stitch towards the right and then pass the needle horizontally underneath, bringing it through at the point where the last stitch passed to the back. The upper needle in the diagram illustrates this movement. Sometimes a single line of this stitching is used (see chevron in Plate XXII); if so it should be worked upon the right side, not starting on the under side as at present. To work the second row of stitching—when the needle has passed the thread to the back at point A, bring it through again six threads to the right, at point B in the diagram. Now reverse the material and start the second row in exactly the same fashion as the first. This second row of stitchery must be at the right distance from the first (see diagram).

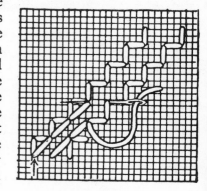

FIG. 158. DIAGONAL CHEVRON (FINAL STAGE).

For the third stage of the working, turn over the fabric and work upon the right side. There should now be upon the surface a double row of zigzag lines as seen in the upper part of figure 158. Bring the thread through at the point marked by the arrow and proceed to work, up the centre, a third line of the stitching exactly like the other two. This line is the simplest to work of the three, for the points of the needle's exit and entrance are all marked out by the working of the first two lines Pull the thread taut whilst working and especially for this third line, for

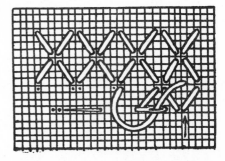

this raises it up. The tight pulling of the other two raised them up on the wrong side and indented them on this side, which throws into more emphasis the raising of the third line. This stitch is effective on both sides of the material.

WINDOW PATTERN FILLING, figure 159.—This filling covers the ground with a series of crossing bars. The diagram explains the working.

FIG. 159. WINDOW PATTERN FILLING.

Successive bands composed of slanting stitches are formed by taking a kind of Back stitch alternately on each side of the narrow band. The needle always picks up five threads of ground material and passes to the back just one thread ahead of the last stitch. Also, when a second row is worked, the needle again carefully leaves a clear thread of fabric between the first and second rows. Thus at the point where four stitches seem to meet, two clear threads of fabric always run between (see diagram). This treatment, together with the usual tight pull on the working thread, draws the material together in parts and leaves little square holes like window-panes recurring at short intervals over the surface. To commence the row there in process of execution, bring the thread through at the point marked by an arrow. Take it to the back at a point diagonally above to the right, passing over three horizontal and two perpendicular threads of ground fabric. Bring it through to the surface, five perpendicular threads farther along towards the left. The

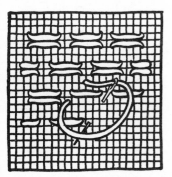

second stitch is passed to the back near where the first stitch commenced (see needle in diagram). The needle is always in a horizontal position when picking up ground fabric. In the diagram it is completing the fourth stitch and some dots point out its further progress along the line.

DOUBLE STITCH FILLING, figure 160. —This filling is similar in the working to Window Pattern, but what was the reverse side there, is, with this, the right side. Consequently the execution is different. The

FIG. 160. DOUBLE STITCH FILLING.

diagram explains it. The needle is working the fourth stitch of a row. For the fifth it picks up a similar diagonal piece of the material, but it points in an upward instead of in a downward direction. This filling looks well upon a pattern arranged with the surface stitches perpendicular, in the diagram they are horizontal. It is sometimes worked with only two threads of fabric between the lines of stitches instead of the three seen here. In the Frontispiece the blue margin is in this stitch.

WAVE STITCH FILLING, figure 161.—This is one of the stitches which are effective worked in coloured threads as well as in white. In

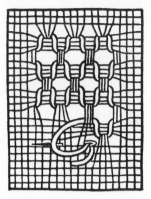

the Frontispiece the water is worked in it in alternate bands of blue and white. The diagram explains the working. The effect to be aimed at is that of an open ground, so the working thread must be pulled taut to bring this about. The needle in the diagram is working the third stitch of the fourth row.

DIAGONAL DRAWN FILLING, figure 162.—This filling can be seen upon a leaf in Plate XX. It is worked diagonally across the fabric. To commence, bring the thread through and then pass the needle to the back four threads above, and bring it to the front again after passing

FIG. 161. WAVE STITCH FILLING.

diagonally under a square composed of four threads in each direction. The needle in the diagram illustrates the working thus far. Next insert the needle at the point where it first came through and bring it out diagonally below after passing under a square of four threads just as before. It is now in position to begin the first process again. When commencing a new row it is necessary to start one thread lower down and one thread more to the right. It is this step lower in each new row which builds up the little crosses seen in the worked sampler, and these give the filling its character.

ROSETTE FILLING, figures 163-165.—This filling covers the surface with a pattern composed of what appear to be tiny rosettes, each one having a raised centre. The rosettes are emphasised by a circle of perforations which occur round their margins. Begin, as with most of these fillings, by imagining the ground fabric divided up into tiny squares measuring three threads in each direction. In the diagram, the ground has been marked out thus with dots. The needle never passes through the material except at these dotted points. The element, or rosette, the repetition of which builds up the pattern, is shown in figure 165, where each straight line represents a stitch and the point where the needle should first come through to the surface is marked by an arrow. When com-

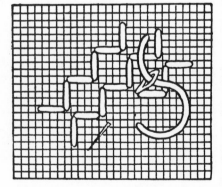

FIG. 162. DIAGONAL DRAWN FILLING.

mencing to work, glance at the larger diagram. In the upper left corner, the execution of the first two stitches is seen, also the needle passing down to the right point for working the second pair. These are similar to the first, but reversed in direction (see key diagram). The first three stitches

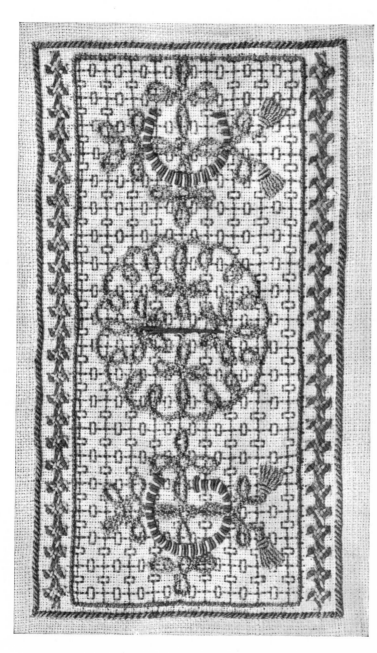

PLATE XXVI. NEEDLE AND THREAD. Letters and needle in Detached
Overcast stitch. Knot work in Double Knot stitch. Interlacing stitch upon bands.

PLATE XXVII. LACE STITCH FILLINGS. *Leaf margins and scrolling stems Overcast Chain. Inner border lines in Double Chain.*

of a rosette can be found in the partly carried out square near the base in the larger diagram. They have been shaded a darker colour than the rest. The numbers in the small working diagram show the order in which to work the different stitches of the rosette, and they are always worked in pairs. The last portion to be worked is the square in the centre, numbered 9 in the diagram. This is raised up by having four tightly pulled Back stitches worked round it. All the stitches must be pulled taut so that they make the necessary perforations and show up the rosette. This is not only done by pulling the thread tightly, but also by so taking the stitches that they are worked like Back stitches, for these by their nature always tend to draw together the fabric threads. It is for this reason that the needle constantly passes

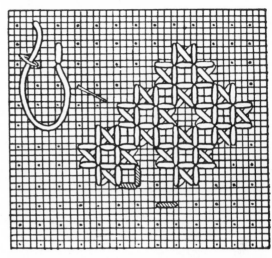

FIG. 163. ROSETTE FILLING.

the thread from one corner to an opposite one and then back again (see numbers in diagram). It is not necessary to keep to this order of working the stitches, for several slightly different ways might do equally well; but having found a good way it is necessary to work each fresh rosette in similar fashion or they will not be alike when done. The rosettes are worked in diagonal lines across a surface. This filling occurs upon a leaf in the corner of Plate XX. Figure 164 shows it with the threads of the ground fabric drawn up as they would be in actual work. Figure 163 only attempts to show the right placing of the stitches.

GREEK CROSS FILLING figure 166.—With this filling the four working stitches take a cruciform shape, but the effect when complete is that of a number of fair-sized perforations repeating regularly over the surface, and the crosses should hardly show. If the working thread

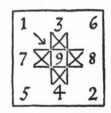

FIG. 165. ROSETTE FILLING (KEY DIAGRAM).

FIG. 164. ROSETTE FILLING AS IT APPEARS WHEN WORKED.

is rightly chosen the stitches will not be too evident. The crosses are worked in diagonal lines upon the surface. Each one is composed of four stitches. The needle in figure 166 is working the second of a group, the first stitch having been shaded to distinguish it from the

K

rest. The order in which the four stitches are worked is noted upon the isolated cross at the base. Each stitch commences in the centre and is worked so that it takes somewhat the form of a Buttonhole stitch. The reason for this is that there must not be any perforation in the centre of the cross, and as the stitches are all pulled tightly there might easily be a space formed there as well as at the four extremities. Each stitch is worked like the one where the needle is. After working the fourth, the needle, instead of coming up again in the centre as before, passes to the centre point of what will be the next cross. A dotted line on the diagram illustrates this, for it marks the passage of the needle from the last cross to the present one in process of being worked. The complete effect of this filling is not obtained until several lines of

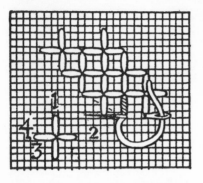

FIG. 166. GREEK CROSS FILLING.

crosses are finished, for then each perforation has four stitches pulling it apart, which makes it much larger than when only the one is pulling at it. When at the end of one diagonal line, it is a simple matter to turn the material round and come up the next line, and then down the third and so on. The filling occurs in Plate XX.

HEM STITCH, figure 167.—The neat line supplied by Hem stitch is the usual finish to the edge of an embroidery. The simplest form of it is illustrated in the diagram. Three warp threads of the ground fabric have been withdrawn, and the hem has been turned in to the edge of the drawn threads. To commence, bring the needle through at the left side. Then pass the thread from right to left, under the first three strands of ground fabric. Pull the thread through and insert the needle in the hem in the manner in process in the diagram, taking care to pick up both hem and fabric underneath. Pull the thread tautly through so as to draw the three strands it has encircled into a tight bunch. The group of threads clustered together can vary in number; for some purposes an even number is more practical. It is sometimes easier to work the Hem stitch with the hem away from the worker; this is the case when a very narrow hem has been formed. The stitch is then executed from left to right, and the rest of the working

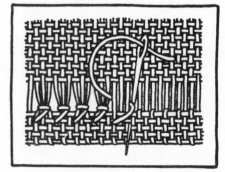

FIG. 167. HEM STITCH.

reversed. With this simple form of Hem stitch only one side of the drawn band is stitched. If more than two warp threads have been withdrawn, it may be necessary to hemstitch both edges. The same stitch can as easily be worked on the opposite edge, and this results in a ladder-like pattern. A chevron pattern is as easily contrived and is worked in much the same fashion. The hem stitching runs along one side, clustering together an even number of threads, say four. Then the second line of Hem stitch is worked on the other side, again gathering up four threads, but the four consist of two from the first and two from the second cluster. By thus splitting the clustered bunches of the upper row a chevron effect is obtained.

WOVEN HEM STITCH, figure 168. —A durable method by which to decorate an open hem is illustrated in the diagram. With the usual hemstitched edge, where the weft threads of the ground fabric are exposed without covering, this portion of the material wears out before the remainder of the

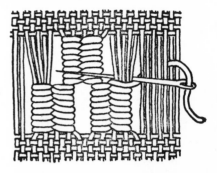

FIG. 168. WOVEN HEM STITCH.

fabric, owing to having lost the support of the warp. But when given the treatment illustrated here—that is, the exposed weft covered with a darning to and fro of new thread—it is perhaps stronger than any other part. To carry out the pattern illustrated in the diagram, draw out the requisite number of threads and proceed to cover them with a kind of weaving stitch. Work with a blunt-pointed needle, and darn the thread to and fro in weaving fashion, alternately over and under two clusters of weft threads each composed of five strands. During this process, draw the threads rather close together so that there is an open space between the clusters. The needle in the diagram is in the act of passing from one cluster to the next. Patterns more complex than this are easily planned. When the difficulty occurs of passing from one cluster to the next, the needle deftly passes the thread invisibly up the centre of the intervening worked cluster. Sometimes, when a band of this kind decorates a hem, it is necessary first to hemstitch the edge before commencing the weaving stitch. Two other patterns in woven Hem stitch are illustrated on the sampler in Plate XXIX.

FIG. 169. DOUBLE HEM STITCH.

DOUBLE HEM STITCH, figure 169. —An ornamental edge is made by this. To execute Double Hem stitch, commence by working a line of ordinary Hem stitch. Then draw out two or three more warp threads beyond, leaving a portion of fabric between the two bands of drawn work. To commence, bring the thread through to the surface at the right-hand end of the line to be stitched (see arrow). Next, pass the needle over these first three threads in the direction from left to right, then back under them, and bring up the working thread at the starting-point. The second stitch can be easily followed in the diagram where the needle is at work. This executed, the first is repeated again and so on. This part of the stitch, without the hemstitched base, is often used alone to work open lines across fabric, not only at margins close to a Hem stitch. For this, usually only a single thread of ground fabric is drawn out on each side of the portion to be worked over.

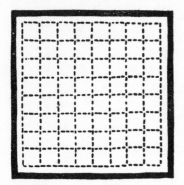

FIG. 170. SQUARE DIVIDED UP BY LINES OF DRAWN STITCHING.

Another stitch for this purpose is shown in figures 149 and 151. A linen cloth can be divided up into a square by working lines of this stitching across at intervals (see figure 170). It might then be decorated with the alternate squares filled in with embroidered sprigs, or with a border.

DRAWN SQUARE, figure 171.—This is a little element for use in white embroidery. It makes a good centre or a repeating unit for a surface or a border. It fills a square composed of twelve threads of fabric in each direction. Commence by overcasting the outer three threads of the square all round. Study of the diagram will show that the first four of these stitches pass into the same perforation at the corner on their inner side, but on their outer, each stitch has a thread of ground fabric between it and the next. The next six overcast stitches are taken so that on both sides they have a thread of ground fabric between each one and the next. The remaining stitches are worked like the first ones. The overcasting of the circle in the centre is treated in much the same way. The diagram shows exactly how the threads of ground fabric are divided by the overcast stitches. (See Plate XXII.)

BARRED BUTTONHOLE WHEEL, figure 172.—It is as easy to work Buttonhole Wheel with a barred centre as in the usual way. Instead of working the sixteen stitches composing it always into the same hole in the centre, work the first four into one interstice of the fabric, then miss over one thread and work four into the next, and continue in the same way round the circle. For a larger wheel, a double bar might be left in the centre.

FIG. 171. DRAWN SQUARE.

FIG. 172. BARRED BUTTONHOLE WHEEL.

EYELET STITCH, figure 173.—There are some kinds of embroidery in which all the stitching is put upon the background, the pattern being left in the plain material and finished off with an outline. The stitch now described is used for working closely over a background in white embroidery. It gives somewhat the effect of a lace ground, for the method of working covers over the surface with closely repeating perforations. The execution is illustrated in the diagram, where one eyelet is completed, another is in process of being made, and dotted lines suggest two more. There should be about twelve divisions round each disc. To commence, bring the needle through at any point on the circumference. Then take a couple of Back stitches upon it, passing, for both stitches, in and out at the same two points. The needle will now have brought the thread through again at the point of starting. Now take a couple more Back stitches, this time passing in at the centre of the circle and out on the circumference. When working the second of these stitches, bring the needle through, instead of at the starting-point, a little farther along on the circumference. This is done in order to be in position for working two more Back stitches in the same way as at the

FIG. 173. EYELET STITCH.

start. All these stitches must be pulled a little tightly, and if they have been put in at the right points, there should result a dozen small perforations round the circumference, each separated from the other by a couple of Back stitches, and a larger one in the centre with a number of stitches radiating from it to the marginal perforations. The second disc is joined on to the first by using two of the latter's perforations in its own circle. A design for which Eyelet stitch is to make the background must be simple in outline and composed of fairly broad masses, in order to make contrast between the plain ground of the pattern and the decorative background. For the same reason there should be a band of plain linen round the margin framing up the completed work, for this doubles the effectiveness of the enriched ground.

CHAPTER IX—BLACK WORK, LACE STITCH FILLINGS AND DARNING

WHEN an embroidery composition contains a number of large leaves and flowers it is often necessary to treat some of these with open, and others with solid fillings, for an occasional lighter treatment gives contrast and relief to the heavier fillings of the rest. Sometimes an open effect is attained by a simple veining, the leaf having no other stitching upon it beyond perhaps a double outline in con-

FIG. 174. STAR FILLING.

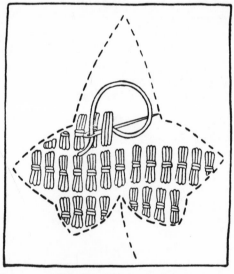

FIG. 175. SHEAF FILLING.

trasted colours. Another way is to cover the surface with some small repeating unit such as those in figures 174 to 178. A third method is to fill in the form with the lace stitches which honeycomb the surface lightly over. Pattern Darning is another pretty treatment for surfaces of this kind. This diapering of the surface can be varied to any extent; it is usually most effective when of an orderly, rather than when of an irregular type. A firm and decided outline is a necessary finish to these fillings. Frequently the little stars and squares of which these patterns are often built up are worked by the counted threads of the ground fabric. When a particularly refined effect is wanted, the pattern should be carried out thus in stitches all of the same length, say, over three threads of the ground fabric. In Plate XXV the patterns are all executed thus.

Working by the counted threads of the ground makes the stitches exactly alike, and it brings the fabric in to help in the composition of the pattern, and this is always, in embroidery, a pleasing treatment—in fact, the more fabric and stitching can be made interdependent the better the result. These geometrical treatments are as useful for the background as for the pattern. Plates XXVI and XXXIV illustrate their application to a ground.

The five open filling patterns illustrated in figures 174–178 need little explanation. The quatrefoil shapes in figure 174 are worked

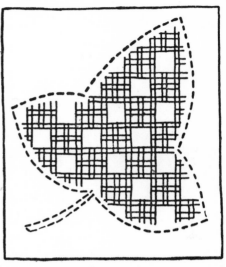

FIG. 176. PLAID FILLING.

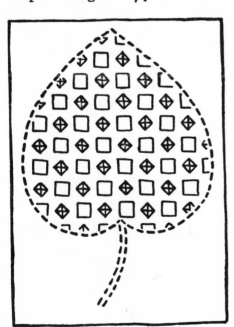

FIG. 177. SQUARE FILLING.

without any previous tracing. A star with eight points is first executed, and then four stitches joining them are put in at the edges. The sheaf filling in figure 175 is of a different type; it is prettier worked in waved rather than in straight lines, and is formed of three upright stitches bound together in the centre by two transverse ones. Figure 176, if required to be worked quickly, can have the long lines thrown across from side to side, but it looks neater if built up with small stitches. The square pattern in figure 177 must be worked on a ground of regular mesh, but with that of figure 178 this is not so necessary. Most of these geometrical fillings, however, are better worked on clearly discerned, even-meshed fabric and with fine thread. As regards colour, black is often used, though other dark colours also look well. Sometimes two or more colours are employed in the one pattern, or they can be worked in light colour upon a dark ground. This geometrical open work was commonly practised in England in the sixteenth century and was said to have been brought by Catherine of Aragon from Spain. It was known as Black work, owing to its being executed in fine black silk. A number of these patterns are given in Plate XXV. The material there used, a fine single canvas, is of a suitable kind to work these fillings upon. They sometimes decorate the background as in Plate XXXIV, or they may fill the pattern as in the headpiece to Chapter VIII. DIAMOND FILLING, figure 179.—This is a stitch used in needle-point lace, but it is equally pretty for embroidery work. To execute it, bring the thread through at the upper right corner of the square and take it to the back at the upper left corner, thus laying a line of thread across the top. Bring the working thread to the front again immediately below where it just passed through. Proceed to tie the working thread to the line of thread at the top corner by a Coral Knot similar to that which is in process of being worked by the needle lower in the diagram. Whilst doing this it is not necessary to pass the needle at the same time through the material,

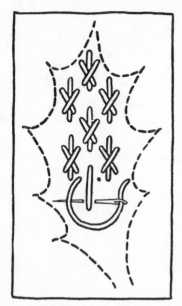

FIG. 178. ERMINE FILLING.

but it can be done, and sometimes the filling is more regular if the needle fixes it in this way at each knotted point. Next, the working thread is again tied by the same knot to the line of thread a little farther along. Between the first and the second knot a loose loop of the working thread must be left, for this has afterwards to be joined by another knot to a line below. This process of alternate loops and knots is continued till the top right-hand corner is reached. After knotting the thread there, the needle passes it to the back and brings it up about an eighth of an inch below in position for casting the second line of thread from side to side. This done, the needle is

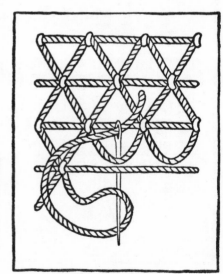

FIG. 179. DIAMOND FILLING.

brought to the front again on the left side just below where it last went through. A second line of knots and loops is now formed and the upper row of loops fixed down at the same time (see needle). In Plate XXXIII the central leaf is filled in by means of this stitch, and on Sampler XXVII all the lace stitches now to be described are to be found.

HONEYCOMB FILLING, figure 180.—The figure illustrates how to execute this light filling. Large centres of flowers and other spaces may often be decoratively worked by this method. To execute the filling, first the rows of horizontal threads are laid across the leaf, then one set of the diagonal lines are laid on top, not threaded in and out, of these. The only interlacement there is comes with the third series of lines. These must be taken across, but during their passage they must pass under the horizontal and over the diagonal lines. In the diagram the needle is working one of these interlaced lines. This final process binds the three series of threads quite firmly together. The threads must cross each other at regular intervals, and in such a fashion that at the point where the

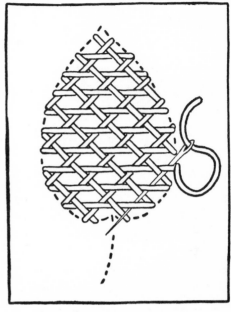

FIG. 180. HONEYCOMB FILLING.

three cross, the threads form a close triangle of interlacement. A new interest to this filling may be added by varying the colour of the different threads; if these are well chosen, a good effect either of harmony or of contrast can be gained.

OPEN BUTTONHOLE FILLING, figure 181.—The filling shown here is an Open Buttonhole stitch, each new row of which is worked into the heading of the row above, and it does not enter the ground fabric except upon touching the circumference of the circle. The needle can, for ease of execution and for stability, pick up the under fabric, but the effect thus gained is not quite similar. Simple alterations in the spacing of the stitches would bring about a number of slightly varying geometrical patterns. Some of these are illustrated in Plate XXVII.

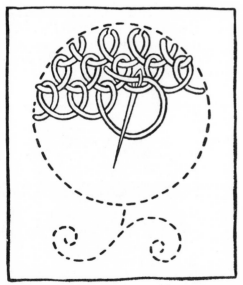

FIG. 181. OPEN BUTTONHOLE FILLING.

SPACED BUTTONHOLE FILLING, figure 182.—A chequered open filling is formed by the aid of Buttonhole and is worked as follows: first two stitches placed close together, then a space, then the two close stitches again and so on. The space left open should fill the same area as the two close stitches. In the illustration, the needle is seen passing the thread into the heading of the row of stitching above. If need be, the needle can, at the same time, pass through the ground fabric. Sometimes this gives more stability, and it also allows the stitches to be larger. A pretty effect is obtained by working alternate rows of different colour.

FANCY BUTTONHOLE FILL-ING, figure 183.—An outline of Chain or Back stitch must first be worked round the form, for into this the stitch is fixed. Examination of the diagram will show that this stitch is a form of buttonholing. To commence the filling, bring the thread through at the left upper corner just outside the backstitched vertical line. Next work an ordinary Buttonhole stitch, looping the thread into the Back stitch line at the top. Then work, close to the first one, a kind of upside-down Button-hole stitch in the manner illustrated by the needle in the diagram. These two stitches are repeated at short intervals along the line to the end, and then the thread is passed under the marginal line and another row of the same stitching worked, but in the contrary direction. For all rows after the first, the stitches are looped into the thread of the preceding row at the part where a loop of thread joins a pair of stitches together. This gives the appearance of a chequer pattern over the filling.

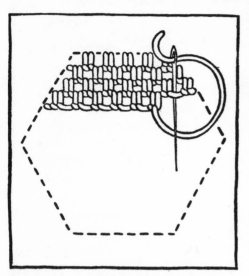

FIG. 182. SPACED BUTTONHOLE FILLING.

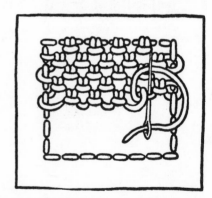

FIG. 183. FANCY BUTTONHOLE FILLING.

KNOTTED BUTTONHOLE FILL-ING, figure 184.—This surface stitch looks well worked in coarse thread. It forms a knotty, irregular surface, which is just what is required for some fillings. Commence by working an outline of Chain or Back stitch round the margin and then bring up the working thread at the left upper corner, and begin the filling by looping a Buttonhole stitch into the top out-line. This done, work a second Buttonhole stitch upon the angle of the first stitch in the manner shown by the needle. Work a series of these double stitches to the end of the line and there pass the thread under the outline and work a line of the same stitches back again to the starting-point. This row will be in the contrary direction, so the button-holing must be reversed.

LACE STITCH FILLING, figure 185.—This lace stitch is a variety of Buttonhole and is worked from left to right. At the end of the line the thread is twisted round the lower portion of the stitch until it reaches the left side again. In the lower corner of the diagram the first row of stitching has been drawn, free from the entanglement of the second row in order that the worker can the more clearly see the method. To commence, a single thread is thrown across the apex and the needle brought through again an eighth of an inch lower down on the left margin of the leaf. The needle in the

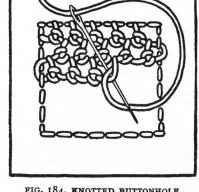

FIG. 184. KNOTTED BUTTONHOLE FILLING.

diagram shows how to continue working the stitch. At the end of the row, pass the thread back to the start by winding it round the base of the worked portion. It passes round, once only, between each stitch. In actual work, the rows of stitches are pulled tautly down when fixing the lowest line which gives the interstices a honeycomb shape. These can be decorated by putting a knot in the centre of each. All these lace fillings can be found upon the sampler in Plate XI, besides some more. Ball stitch (figure 92) occurs upon one leaf and Twisted Lattice (figure 99) and Diamond (figure 48) upon others. The rest are chiefly variations upon figure 102. Instead of working the simple chequering of two together and a space some other sequence is followed. For example the leaf

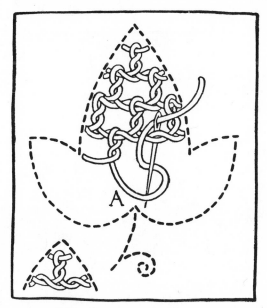

FIG. 185. LACE STITCH FILLING.

occurring at the top left corner is worked as follows. First a row of spaced single Buttonhole, then one of spaced Buttonhole grouped two together. The third row returns to the order of the first and the fourth to that of the second. Other variations of a like kind occur upon the rest. The worker will easily devise new ones.

THE DIFFERENT FORMS OF DARNING USED IN EMBROIDERY, figures 186-191.

—The darning used in embroidery may be divided into two kinds. The one is of a bold type suitable for carrying out work on a large scale, using coarse threads. This is sometimes

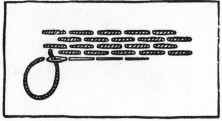

FIG. 186. DARNING.

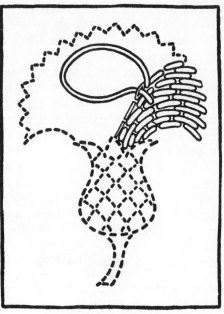

FIG. 187. DARNING.

the only method employed for the execution of a large design, both pattern and ground being solidly filled in by its means. The direction taken by the lines of stitching is important, for this, together with colour and tone, form the chief attraction of the work. The other is a finer kind of work, usually executed in split floss or similar thread, and it aims at a different effect from the other. In all darning work the stitch is alike. It is a running one which picks up at short intervals just one thread of ground material. With the execution, however, the likeness between the two ceases, for the type of design employed and the general character of the work is opposed. Figures 186 and 187 illustrate darning stitch. With all forms of decorative darning it is usual to pick up with the needle as small a piece of material as possible, otherwise the requisite effect, that of an all-over silky surface, will be in part lost. For the same reason the successive lines of stitching must lie close to each other so that no ground peeps through between. The material used for the background affects the technique, so it is important to choose a suitable one. The ground stuff, usually linen or cotton, should be fairly fine and of a loosely woven texture in order that the separate threads may be easily seen and picked up. Sometimes the

FIG. 188. A DARNED BACK-GROUND.

lines of stitching are made to follow the outline of the design in the manner shown in figures 187 and 188. A quick way of darning a background is to place the lines of stitching slightly apart instead of touching each other, for this it may be necessary to use a ground stuff that looks well, besides being practical. Irregular darning may decorate a ground with bands of alternate colour. For example, the design which forms the headpiece to Chapter I could be treated thus. The flowers would be worked only in outline. The stitches should be as near as possible of the same length, and the thread, often a coarse twisted silk, should not untwist in the working. The type of design chosen for this bolder kind of darning must be simple in outline and not too small in its detail.

PATTERN DARNING, figures 189, 190, 194.—Darning in pattern is contrived by picking up the threads of the ground material in some regular sequence, with the result that a simple geometrical pattern is displayed upon the surface. This method involves a certain amount of counting of the ground threads, but this is not so tedious, for after the first few rows are completed hardly any counting is necessary. Figure 189 illustrates some pattern darning in progress. A chevron ground is being worked behind

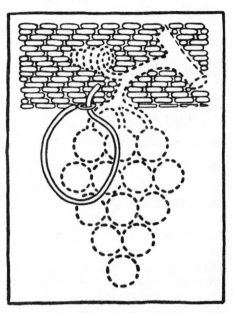

FIG. 189. PATTERN DARNING.

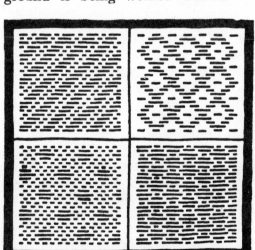

FIG. 190. DESIGNS FOR PATTERN DARNING.

the pattern, which will be executed afterwards in outline only. This fine kind of darning is often used for the enrichment of backgrounds, for, owing to its quiet, monotonous character, it is well suited to such a purpose. To carry out the diagram, commence the darning at the top, and take a line of stitching horizontally across, picking up alternately one thread and passing over about four. For the second line, which can be run in the opposite direction, pick up the threads as before, but start with the first stitch a step ahead of the first one of the previous row. This goes on for five rows and then the ground thread, for five more rows, is picked up a step behind the same one of the row before. By varying the order and the quantity of stuff when picking up the thread, all kinds of simple repeating patterns can be displayed. Figures 190, 194 and the headpiece of this chapter show some of these. Figure 194 can be copied easily, for it shows every thread of the ground fabric.

DAMASK DARNING, figures 191, 192.—Pattern darning can be fur-

FIG. 191. CENTRE PORTION OF A DAMASK DARN.

ther complicated by running the threads in two opposed directions. This is most simply explained by an illustration. Figure 192 shows a simple darn with the thread taken in both perpendicular and horizontal directions. If two suitable colours are used for this, a charming effect of shot damask silk is obtained in the centre. There are in existence a number of old samplers, of early nine-

FIG. 192. DAMASK DARNING.

teenth-century date, filled with most exquisite fine darns of this kind, worked in colours in every imaginable patterning. These were in all probability executed partly to practise fine darning for mending damask table linens and also as an exhibition of skill. Figure 191 illustrates the central portion only of a damask darn. The fabric is often cut away under this portion of the work. Figure 192 can be used to work from, for in it the threads of the ground can be counted. Plate XXVIII displays upon the background a number of patterns in darning. The darning thread runs from side to side of each panel passing under the animal on its way across.

DOUBLE DARNING, figure 193.—There is yet another form of darning which is occasionally required. This is Double Darning and its special characteristic lies in its being alike

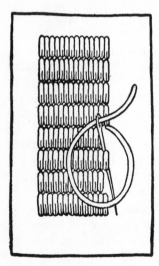

FIG. 193. DOUBLE DARNING.

on both sides of the ground fabric, for some purposes a useful quality. The method is found in use upon work coming from the Near East, Persia, Asia Minor, Turkey, and the Greek islands. The stitch consists in the first place of a running which picks up exactly as much fabric as it leaves. At the end of a line the needle commences to return to the starting-point and on this journey picks up the fabric it left untouched before. The needle should pass in and out at the same points as on the first journey. In the diagram the needle has almost completed a

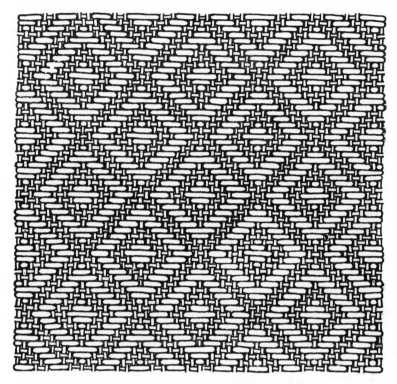

FIG. 194. A DESIGN FOR PATTERN DARNING.

return journey. This kind of darning is sometimes seen carrying out a pattern which gives an effect of horizontal bands across the surface as in the diagram, at other times it is worked so as to pattern the form with diagonal bands. The latter way is contrived by making each fresh line start a step higher or lower than the previous row. A common practice is to make each fresh line start exactly half-way up the previous one. Of the four kinds of darning described in this chapter, namely, Irregular, Pattern, Damask and Double Darning, Pattern is the most useful and perhaps the most effective kind for embroidery purposes.

CHAPTER X—CUT AND DRAWN WORK AND INSERTION STITCHES

THE method of work by which the ground fabric in certain parts is cut away and the resulting spaces filled with foliage, geometrical figures, inscriptions or other fanciful devices, is one which has great possibilities. By its means much beautiful work has been done in the past. The early English samplers often exhibit strips of fine cut work. The inspiration for these probably came from Italy, for that country has always excelled in this particular branch of needlework. There are in existence a number of Italian and some English sixteenth-century pattern books filled with designs for cut work which show how popular it was at that period. The design, to be effective, must be bold and simple even though the work is of small compass and fine, as it usually is. Some embroidery upon the surrounding solid parts adds a finish to the open spaces. Plate XXIX would have appeared bald and incomplete without the fragments of decoration round about its open squares. A larger piece of a similar kind of decoration is illustrated in Plate XXII; it is a suitable type to combine with cut work. The fabric chosen for the ground must be practical for working upon, or difficulty will be encountered with frayed or clumsy

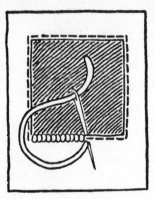

FIG. 195. OVERCAST EDGE.

edges. Fine hand-made linen, if it does not fray too easily, has the best appearance. The working thread should be similar to the threads of the ground fabric, as much so as to give the impression that when weaving the linen the threads had changed their direction and twisted up into pattern instead of continuing to weave plain fabric.

OVERCAST EDGE, figure 195.—To overcast a cut edge is the neatest form of securing it. The diagram illustrates a square with the four sides cut away and an Overcast stitch in process of binding the edge. Before cutting out the square a line of thread should be run round it. This ties it in, thus preventing any stretching of the edges during the after work, and gives the overcast line more emphasis, by slightly raising it. When, owing to a frayable material, it is not a safe plan first to cut the actual edges of the open work, there are alternative methods of treatment; these are described next. The use of fine needles and fine thread often saves a cut edge from fraying during the working. Also to avoid the same danger, the four edges of a square need not all be cut out at the start, one or two sides may be cut first and then overcast before the remaining two are exposed.

LOOPED EDGE, figure 196.—The diagram illustrates another edging stitch and another method of treating the cut edges. This stitch has a firm heading into which it is easily possible to work various lace stitches for filling the open space. This edging is useful when a filling of this kind is contemplated, for it is firmer than Buttonhole for such a purpose. The needle explains the method of work. Hold the material in a position so that the edge to be worked is nearest the worker. Insert the needle into the edge from the underside upwards. When the

FIG. 196. LOOPED EDGE.

thread is nearly pulled through, pass the needle through the loop as shown in the diagram. Then, when pulling the last piece of thread tight, let needle and thread point away from the worker. Care must be taken where the start and finish meet that no sign of junction is visible. This figure illustrates an alternative method of treating the cut edge when fine ground fabric is in use. The square of linen is cut from corner to corner and turned back underneath. The edging stitch is worked upon the folded linen, and when finished the linen can be cut away on the underside, close to the stitching. This makes a durable edge that will stand much wear and

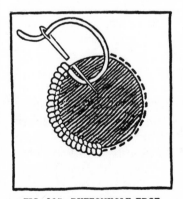

FIG. 197. BUTTONHOLE EDGE.

tear. With coarse fabric it is too clumsy a method to employ.

BUTTONHOLE EDGE, figure 197.—A usual form of securing the raw edges in cut work is by Buttonhole. Both Ordinary and Tailor's Buttonhole are used; the former makes a narrower edge. Edges are sometimes buttonholed before being cut away. A thread is first run round to mark the line, the Buttonhole stitch worked over it, and then, with sharp scissors, ones having well curved points by choice, the linen is cut away quite close to the buttonholing. It should be cut so cleanly that no after trimming up is necessary, for when this has been done, the edge is never so clean as when completed at the first incision. The diagram illustrates a cut circle being edged with the usual form of Buttonhole.

THE FILLINGS FOR THE CUT SPACES, figures 198–200.—As a general rule the fillings for cut work are executed by the three stitches illustrated in figures 199–200. There are besides a number of Lace

L

stitch fillings (see pages 110–113); these are a distinct kind of work more nearly allied to lace. Figure 199 illustrates Buttonhole stitch being worked over a bar. The upper bar shows a single row of stitches worked

FIG. 198. DESIGN FOR CUT WORK.

FIG. 199. BUTTONHOLED BAR.

FIG. 200. WOVEN AND OVERCAST BARS.

slightly apart, and the lower one, where the needle is at work, shows the completion of the bar by a second line of buttonholing, on the opposite side, so arranged that its stitches fit in between those of the first row. The bars which are covered by the Buttonhole consist of some threads of the ground material which have been left uncut when the rest of the ground was removed. These bars, when possible, should be actual threads of the original fabric. Sometimes, for instance when they occur diagonally, this is not possible, and then they have to be made by throwing the thread to and fro several times. These thrown threads are then covered over with stitching. This Buttonhole covering stitch is used when the bar is going to be widened on each side, for any number of fresh rows of buttonholing can be worked into the heading of the row before. By this simple means many varieties of forms can be built up in the cut spaces, for example, leaves, flower petals, or geometrical shapes. When the bar is completed by one row of stitching, no others having to be added on either edge, it is usual to cover it either with a single line of close Buttonhole, or one of the two stitches illustrated

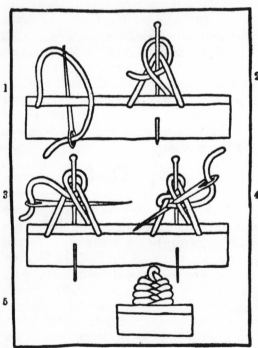

FIG. 201. WOVEN PICOT.

in figure 200. These are a kind of weaving to and fro, and an over-casting. The overcasting makes the narrowest bar. The woven one makes a firm flat band. Both are easily done and are explained

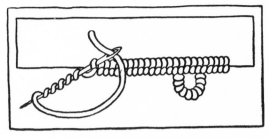

FIG. 202. BULLION PICOT.

by the diagram. The needle at work on the woven bar picks up half the bundle of threads, first on one side and then on the other, taking care to keep the thread even by pulling it equally tightly each time. The completed bar should be of the same width from start to finish. Figure 198 shows a design for a small square, various others can be seen in Plate XXIX and figure 206.

WOVEN PICOT, figure 201.—Buttonhole bars are frequently decorated by the addition of Picots. This is the largest of the present group. A

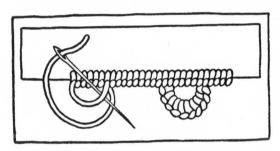

FIG. 203. RING PICOT.

completed sample can be seen at the base of the diagram. Commence by making a loop on the edge of the fabric as shown in the upper left corner. Next fix the loop thus formed with a pin as shown in the next diagram, and make a second loop round the pin. Pass the needle across under the loop as in diagram 3. Now bring the thread back to the left side again, passing in front of the loop, and on the way, pick up with the needle the thread which has just passed underneath (see fourth diagram). The two stages shown in the second band are repeated as many times as necessary to fill in the picot.

BULLION PICOT, figure 202.—Bullion stitch makes a pretty picot. The Bullion Knot is worked in the usual way, but attached to the edge of the Buttonhole stitch instead of to the ground fabric. To commence, insert the needle in the thread of the

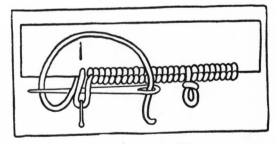

FIG. 204. LOOP PICOT.

edging stitch, wind as many loops round it as the size of picot requires, pull the needle through the loops and insert it again at the same point in the edging stitch and pull through. To make this picot more open in form, like the completed one in the diagram, commence by picking up about three of the edging stitches with the needle instead of one. Then at the finish, pass the needle through these a second time.

RING PICOT, figure 203.—A large picot is made by working Buttonhole stitch over a semicircular loop of thread. This is illustrated in the

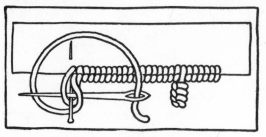

FIG. 205. BUTTONHOLE PICOT.

diagram. Here ordinary Buttonhole is being worked over the thread, but Overcast stitch or Tailor's Buttonhole might be substituted in place of it. At the required point, the thread is looped backwards into the heading of the edging stitch and then overcast or buttonholed back to the starting-point. If a stouter semi-circle is wanted, pass the thread three times to and fro instead of once.

LOOP PICOT, figure 204.—This is the simplest form of picot. The method of work is shown in the diagram, which illustrates both a completed picot and one in process of being made. It consists of a loop made firm at the base by a Buttonhole stitch worked across it. Upon reaching the required point insert a pin in the edge of the fabric. Pass the working thread under the pin, then into the edge of the fabric, and then work a Single Buttonhole stitch across the base of the loop thus formed.

BUTTONHOLE PICOT, figure 205.—A small picot, a development of the last described one, is illustrated here. It is worked in similar fashion to the one just described. After passing the working thread round the

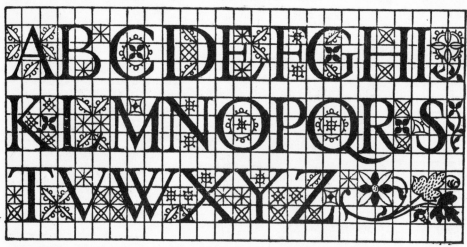

FIG. 206. DECORATED ALPHABET FOR CUT WORK, FROM A SIXTEENTH-CENTURY PATTERN BOOK.

pin and again into the fabric, pass the needle up through the centre of the loop round the pin a second time, and then work three or four Buttonhole stitches upon the loop. This process will bring the thread down to the right position for continuing the edging stitch.

Figure 206 is a design for cut work taken from an Italian late sixteenth-century pattern book. A seventeenth-century English sampler, worked with a similar alphabet, carried out in the most minute cut work patterns, can be seen in the Victoria and Albert Museum.

RUSSIAN OVERCAST FILL-ING, figure 207.—This and the next described stitch are often used together to work a pattern. Plate XXX is executed entirely by their means. The design, copied from a piece of Russian work, is an example of neat planning, for both pattern and background take equally inter-esting forms. To commence working a band like this, first withdraw two, and then leave two, fabric threads in each direction, and then overcast the cut edges of the square. Begin by overcasting the threads which lie beneath the pattern. How to do this is illustrated in the diagram. The overcasting is carried out in zigzag diagonal lines, two stitches passing over horizontal threads, one across the diagonal and then two across perpendicular threads, and so on. In figure 207 two diagonal working lines have been commenced in order to show how they work together.

FIG. 207. RUSSIAN OVERCAST FILLING.

At the point of junction two working threads pass across the same square of fabric threads.

RUSSIAN DRAWN FILLING, figure 208.—The portion of fabric in Plate XXX not covered with Russian Overcast is worked in this stitch. Like the other part it is exe-cuted in diagonal lines and just two rows of it together as seen in the sampler make a particularly satis-factory pattern, though it can be used for an entire filling. Figure 208 explains the working. Bring the thread through at the perforation marked by an arrow, carry it across two bars, then back over itself and under and over the fabric threads, bringing it to

FIG. 208. RUSSIAN DRAWN FILLING.

the surface again in position for working the second stage of the stitch. In the diagram a completed stitch can be seen on the left, whilst the two stages which work it are shown separately above. These two would in the actual work lie one across the other. The diagram shows the working of the two stages, also how to pass to the next square to commence the second stitch. Russian Drawn filling is not effective unless just the right material and thread is chosen to work it. That used in the sampler Plate XXX is of a suitable kind.

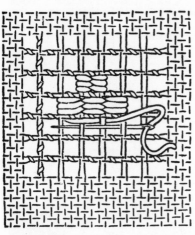

FIG. 209. WEAVING STITCH FILLING.

WEAVING STITCH FILLING, figure 209.—This is an effective method of work, and both simple and quick in execution. Commence by withdrawing certain of the fabric threads. In the diagram the sequence followed is one withdrawn and two left in alternation. The exact number depends upon the mesh of the fabric and the size of the working thread. Next lightly overcast the exposed fabric threads, at first only those lying in a horizontal direction. The weaving to and fro of the pattern is then executed, and finally the perpendicular threads of any fabric still exposed are lightly overcast. These are not overcast at first because they are better left free under the woven portion. Any pattern based on squares, such as most of the canvas work ones, can be copied by this method, though some are more practical than others for it. Plate XXXI has the central and right-hand square worked in it. The central one takes the weaving in two directions, which gives a pretty damask-like effect to the design, for the light catches it in different ways and gives different tones to the surface.

LINEN FILLING.—In the square to the left of the centre in Sampler XXXI the design is left in the linen ground, instead of, like the opposite one, having it put in by after stitching. For this the edge of the design is first neatly overcast. Sometimes run lines of thread mark it out in the first place and the overcasting is taken over these run lines of thread. This raises the edge a little. Next the necessary threads of fabric are cut and withdrawn in the same way as for the other square. The exposed threads of fabric are now closely overcast with fine thread.

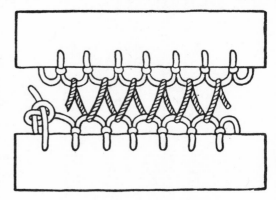

FIG. 210. LACED INSERTION STITCH.

LACED INSERTION STITCH, figures 210, 211.—The diagram illustrates an insertion stitch, which is easily unfastened or joined up. If, however, more stability is required than is given by the simple laced thread, it would be quite easy to combine the Knotted Insertion stitch, figure 212,

PLATE XXVIII. PATTERN DARNING. *Backgrounds*
Pattern Darned, divided by Guilloche stitch. Margin in Pekinese.

PLATE XXIX. DRAWN THREAD AND CUTWORK.

PLATE XXX. DRAWN THREAD PANEL. In Russian Drawn
and Overcast Fillings. Marginal lines in Chequered Chained Border.

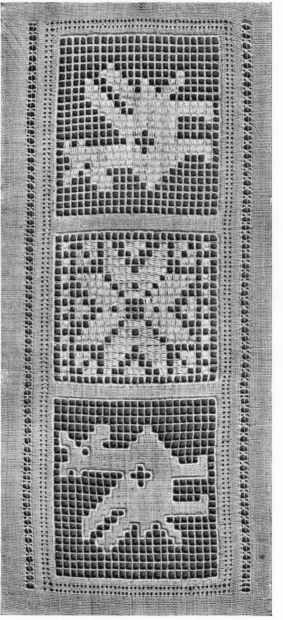

PLATE XXXI. DRAWN THREAD SQUARES in Linen filling and Weaving stitch filling.

with this one and join the edges with the firmly knotted thread. To carry out this stitch, the first process is to work upon both edges the looped stitch illustrated in the diagram. This, known as Braid Edging stitch, figure 211, is worked in very similar fashion to Braid stitch, figure 69, although when completed it does not much resemble it. Commence by placing the edge of the material, which is to be bound, away from the worker, and work from right to left. Pass the needle with the loop round it under the edge of the material, and bring it to the surface as if working a buttonholed edge. When pulling the thread through, in order to tighten the knot, it should be drawn out in the direction away from the worker. This gathers up the knot on the actual edge. The knot, in process of being pulled tight, can be seen in figure 210, at the end of one of the lines where it has been left loose.

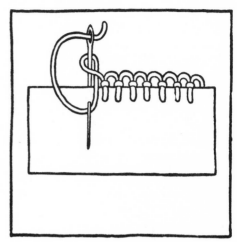

FIG. 211. BRAID EDGING STITCH.

Braid Edging is a most satisfactory binding stitch, for it looks equally neat whether seen from the upper or under side or from the actual edge. The final lacing through to complete the insertion is done when, both edgings finished, the two materials have been firmly fixed to a temporary backing.

KNOTTED INSERTION STITCH, figure 212.—The diagram illustrates Antwerp Edge adapted as an insertion. It is very practical for the purpose, for the constantly recurring knot makes the edge firm and strong. The needle carries the thread from edge to edge alternately, and after taking it through the material, always in the direction from above downwards, it ties a simple knot in the thread close to the edge of the material. The edges to be joined must be kept firmly in place whilst the joining stitch is in progress, or the width of the insertion will vary and look irregular. A good plan is to tack both edges upon

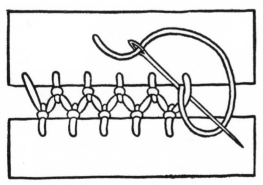

FIG. 212. KNOTTED INSERTION STITCH.

a temporary backing. *Toile cirée* is good, for its shiny surface prevents the needle accidentally piercing it. The insertion joining the stitch samplers in Plate VIII is made up of a combination of figures 211 and 212.

TWISTED INSERTION STITCH, figure 213.—This is a commonly

used insertion, quickly worked and effective, but it is hardly appropriate for adding to good embroidery, as there are many much more interesting forms of insertion than this. The needle in the diagram explains the working. The action there seen in progress is repeated on each edge in turn.

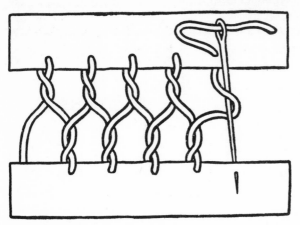

FIG. 213. TWISTED INSERTION STITCH.

ITALIAN BUTTON-HOLE INSERTION STITCH, figure 214.— A strong and decorative insertion stitch is illustrated in the diagram. In Plate VII this is employed to join two parts together. To work the stitch, begin by tacking down the sides, which are to be joined, to some firm backing. Bring the thread to the surface at the edge of the right-hand side strip at the top. Take it to the back on the other strip opposite, and proceed to work about

five Buttonhole stitches along the thread now joining the edges of fabric together. This done, pick up with the needle the edge of the fabric at point A, and then carry the needle and thread across to the left side and pick up the edge of the fabric at point B. This point is not opposite A, it is slightly lower down. Now proceed to work three Buttonhole stitches on the doubled thread which first passed from the uppermost buttonholed bar to the right side, point A, and then was carried across to point B. The needle in the diagram is just commencing to work three such stitches lower down. This button-holing is always worked from the centre towards an edge. These completed, the needle next picks up the edge of the fabric on the right side, a little below point A,

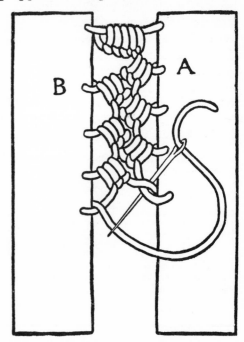

FIG. 214. ITALIAN BUTTONHOLE INSERTION STITCH.

and then works three Buttonhole stitches upon the double bar, which passes between point B and the completed buttonhole stitching above. These three stitches are worked from right to left instead of in the usual direction. Next, the edge of the fabric on the left side is picked up a little below point B, and then the Buttonhole stitches worked on the opposite side as before. In the diagram the needle is in the act of continuing the stitch at the point just reached in the description.

INTERLACING INSERTION, figure 215.—A decorative insertion is built up by Interlacing stitch. This is illustrated in the diagram and the method of working is described in detail on pages 63, 64. To

FIG. 215. INTERLACING INSERTION.

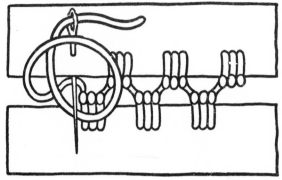

FIG. 216. BUTTONHOLE INSERTION STITCH.

work this as an insertion, tack the two edges of material upon a firm backing about a quarter of an inch apart. Then work the foundation stitching upon the edges of the material to be joined. After this is done complete the interlacement as described on page 64. It is as easy to arrange for three or four rows of this insertion as for one, for it only requires a wider foundation of threads latticed across and several bands

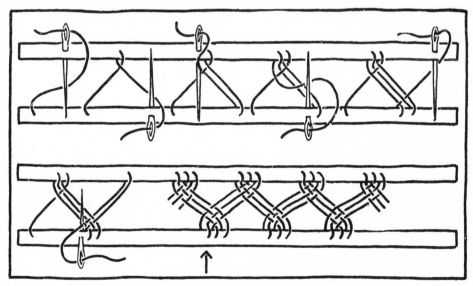

FIG. 217. PLAITED INSERTION STITCH.

of the surface interlacing instead of one. Several rows of Interlacing insertion make a good filling for the open spaces in cut work.

BUTTONHOLE INSERTION STITCH, figure 216.—Both forms of Buttonhole, either Tailor's or ordinary make an effective insertion stitch.

The diagram illustrates Tailor's, as that is the more complicated and stronger one of the two. The way to work this is described on page 25, and figure 216 explains how to adapt it as an insertion.

PLAITED INSERTION, figure 217.—This is a pretty stitch for joining strips of embroidery together, for the plaited chevron line it builds up is an ornament in itself. To execute it, copy the diagram commencing at the top left-hand corner. After having executed the six successive stages illustrated there, continue by commencing at the first again. It will probably be helpful after working the sixth stage to study the completed portion of the insertion which is drawn out in the lower portion of the diagram. In it the point reached at stage six is marked by an arrow, and it is as easy to follow the afterworking in this finished portion as to return to following out the various stages from the starting-point onwards. To gain the best effect work with a coarse firm thread.

CHAPTER XI—COUCHING AND LAID WORK

LAID WORK, figures 218–221.—When commencing a piece of laid work, one of the first questions to be settled is, what means shall be employed to tie down the long strands of thread lying across the surface, which by reason of their length are not, without some such fastening, sufficiently firmly attached to the ground fabric. It is a beautiful treatment of silk, this of laying it flatly down in rather

loose, untwisted strands over the surface of the pattern. For owing to the silk not being cut up into minute lengths by stitches, its smooth glossy texture is shown to full advantage. Laid and couched work, the two are nearly related, are methods often chosen for use together when working with both silk and gold threads. Gold thread makes a good finish to laid work when used as an outline to it, or when employed to assist in the tying down. Laid work, always done with the aid of a frame, is quick in execution. The threads should be laid down loosely, for a strained effect is unpleasant; this is especially the case when it is composed of floss silk. Perhaps to obtain the most artistic result, the

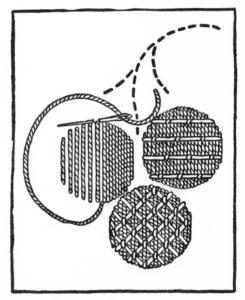

FIG. 218. LAID WORK.

less the tying down thread shows, the better, though at times a special feature is made of this fixing process. Sometimes this thread is of distinct colour, or it is made to follow out some decorative pattern such as those displayed in figures 219 and 220. The laid strands of silk may be of flat colour or exquisitely shaded, also distinct contrasts of colour can be introduced. In the accompanying illustrations, some of the chief methods of executing laid work are shown. In figure 218, upon the berry on the left side, the needle is laying the preliminary threads. It first passes across the surface laying alternate lines of thread, then, as it returns back to the starting-point, fills up the intervening spaces. By laying the threads in this fashion they lie more evenly together because a larger piece of ground fabric can be picked up, for laid threads are never treated like Satin stitch where there is as much thread upon the under as upon the upper side. When the surface to be filled in is covered with even, close parallel lines of thread, the next process is to make it more secure by throwing other lines of thread across at intervals in a contrary direction, and tying each of these as it is laid, with one or two cross stitches (see right-hand berry). Another method of fastening down the underlay is displayed in the lowest berry where a regular trellis is formed by the fixing threads. This method makes such pretty decoration that it is frequently used for the cup of an acorn, the sheath of a thistle,

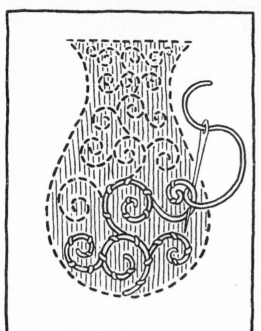

FIG. 219. SCROLL COUCHING UPON LAID THREADS.

and other such subjects. In figure 221 the laid threads are set longitudinally down the leaf and the tying-down thread carries out the veining. Figure 220 illustrates a form of tying down known as scale couching. This is a decorative treatment and it suggests certain forms of natural growth particularly well. In figure 219 the tying-down thread runs up the figure in scroll form, and covers the vase with a simple pattern. There is another method by which laid threads are sometimes secured, which is not illustrated here. This is by working Split stitch across in contrary direction to the underlay. This stitch has been explained on page 50, and the

FIG. 220. SCALE COUCHING UPON LAID THREADS.

only further direction necessary to be given when it is used upon laid work is that the stitches must be quite long, for the less the underlay is split by the passage to and fro of surface threads, the better the effect.

PLATE XXXII. INTERLACING KNOTWORK. In narrow white tape couched with black cotton on a grey linen ground. Flowers in Rosette Chain.

PLATE XXXIII. *Miscellaneous examples.*

COUCHING, figures 222–224.—The tying down of one or more threads upon the material by means of another one is called couching. Some threads are too coarse, too brittle or too delicate to pass constantly to and

fro through the ground stuff, and so this method has been evolved to overcome the difficulty. The problem with couching is to make the tying-down stitch strong enough for it to answer its purpose and yet not spoil the appearance of the surface with too many or too coarse stitches, and especially is this necessary when either gold or silver threads are in use. The mediæval workers solved the problem by inventing a most ingenious method which was both practical and beautiful, and in the middle ages it was used universally for all kinds of couching in both silk and gold thread. A detailed explanation of this almost obsolete method is given later.

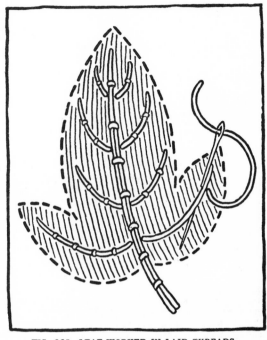

FIG. 221. LEAF WORKED IN LAID THREADS.

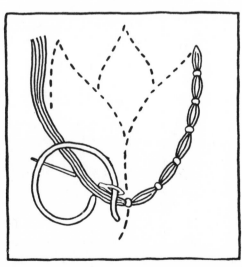

FIG. 222. COUCHING.

There are some other methods of couching besides the straightforward one of fixing threads in place by means of a single transverse stitch as in figure 222. For instance, many ordinary embroidery stitches may be used for the purpose. The fixing-down stitch may require to be invisible. This is the case sometimes when couching down cord, and then the needle must be inserted in between the twists. The diagram illustrates the most direct and simple method of fastening either single or clusters of threads to the material. It is done by passing another thread, which comes to and fro through the material, across the laid threads as shown in the diagram. The tying-down thread may be of contrasting colour or material, and it may occur at regular or irregular intervals or in pattern. Sometimes two couching threads are

M

placed near together and then a longer interval and so on. When clusters of threads are couched down together they are often laid loosely on the material and the fixing-down thread pulled fairly tight. This results in a pretty bunching of the laid threads between the fixed points (see diagram). Ordinary couching is useful for solid fillings, for outline work, for edging applied or laid work and so forth. But one of its chief uses is to fix gold and silver threads in place, for these cannot in the ordinary way be pulled to and fro through the material. Most forms of couching demand the help of a frame. A number of fancy methods of couching down threads are shown in figures 223 and 224.

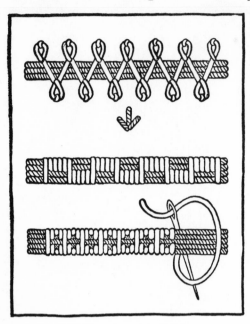

FIG. 223. FANCY COUCHING.

COUCHING BY MEANS OF EMBROIDERY STITCHES, figure 225.—Many stitches can be used for tying down surface threads. Some particularly suitable ones are, Open Chain, Ladder, varieties of Feather, Open Double Back, Buttonhole, Chevron, in fact, most broad open stitches which only enter the material at their edges are suitable. Buttonhole is more used than any other. A buttonhole couched filling (see figure 225) is a very pretty treatment for a leaf or flower petal. To

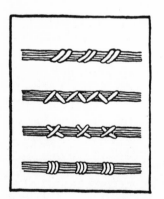

FIG. 224. FANCY COUCHING.

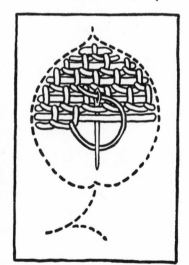

FIG. 225. COUCHING BY MEANS OF BUTTONHOLE STITCH.

work the leaf in the diagram several strands of silk are threaded together in the needle and brought through on the right-hand margin of the leaf near the apex. The threads are then passed across to the opposite margin where they enter the material and come up again immediately below. A row of open buttonholing is next worked across the laid thread from left to right, and when the other margin is reached the laid threads are again passed right across the leaf as before. The needle need not pierce the ground material excepting at the edges, for the filling lies flatter thus treated. The lines of stitching do not always go straight across the form; they may go either up or down, slanting, or following round the outline.

Their direction is as a rule governed by the arrangement of the shading, for the simplest way to shade is to change the colour when commencing a fresh row. Besides fillings, lines of buttonhole couching are useful either as borders or to couch down applied work.

ROUMANIAN COUCH-ING, figure 226.—Another form of couching is illustrated here which is used for covering up broad surfaces. The needle brings the thread through on the left margin, carries it across and to the back upon the right. Then, on its way back to lay a second long thread, it secures the first with one or more cross stitches (see the needle). These stitches must not be at all tight, and should

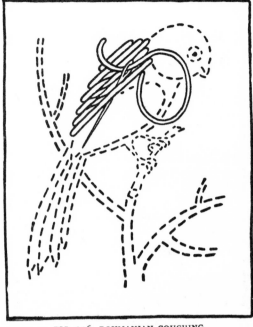

FIG. 226. ROUMANIAN COUCHING.

be taken in a slanting direction, for they are laid thus in order not to be noticeable. In the form of couching illustrated in figure 227 a similar method of execution is described, but in this case its special character lies in the crossing stitch being tightly worked, with the result that it does not in the least resemble the method here illustrated.

BOKHARA COUCHING, figure 227.—The diagram shows a method of couching down silk for solid fillings. It is commonly seen worked in this manner upon Persian embroideries where it covers large expanses with a flat monotonous surface, very pleasing in effect. It looks best worked in coarse untwisted silk. The silk is laid, a line at a time, from side to side of the space to be covered, and then is couched down by slanting stitches taken in regular order across the laid line. These couching stitches must be placed fairly near together and in such a position that they

FIG. 227. BOKHARA COUCHING.

build up slanting lines across the surface (see diagram). The tying down stitch should be tight and the laid silk between a little slack, for this gives the right effect to the finished work.

THE COUCHING OF GOLD THREAD, figures 228–232 —Some of

the best forms of Couching with metal threads are illustrated in the following five diagrams. A particularly good method is shown in figure 228. The gold, usually very fine, is couched two threads at a time up and down the surface. At certain arranged intervals the couching stitches are spaced much farther apart, and by this simple means such a pattern as that seen in

FIG. 228. ITALIAN METHOD OF COUCHING GOLD.

the drawing can be displayed. Instead of the flower seen there, any other, say a geometrical pattern, can be pictured. Leaving the gold thread for an interval, not fastened down, makes it spring up and catch the light, and this throws the pattern into relief. A commonly used method of couching gold is shown in figure 229. The gold, laid in horizontal lines, is tied down two threads together and the tying-down silk is made to follow a lattice pattern. A variation upon this is seen in figure 230. Here the gold is laid in waving lines and spaced a little more openly. This method causes a pretty play of light upon the metal thread. String is sometimes laid under the couched gold to raise it up. In figure 231 it is laid in regular lines across the surface and the gold taken up and down across it so as to build up a basket-like pattern. In figure 232 the string underlay takes a lozenge or diamond shape. For this there must always

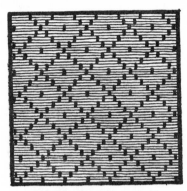

FIG. 229. LATTICE PATTERN.

FIG. 230. WAVED GOLD.

be a couching stitch upon each side of the raised parts to make the line sharp and clear. The oval at the top of Plate XXXIII is worked somewhat in the manner of figure 228. The difference between them is that the pattern, instead of being left to show in raised gold, is closely oversewn with coloured silks. This method is known as *or nué*.

ANCIENT METHOD OF COUCHING, figures 233–238.—In the thirteenth century the method of couching now to be described was practically the only one used. Though nowadays hardly known, it has many

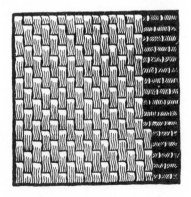

FIG. 231. BASKET PATTERN.

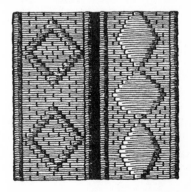

FIG. 232. GOLD COUCHED OVER STRING.

advantages over the more modern method. The work is more durable, the surface more flexible, and the effect much finer. These characteristics were invaluable when the entire gold ground of a cope—a vestment which hangs in graceful folds from the shoulder—was to be couched with gold thread in this manner. And this treatment of the ground of an embroidered cope was a common practice in the Middle Ages. Figure 239 is a fragment from one such vestment. The chevroned

pattern upon the ground is couched in gold. The subject is S. Lawrence
and S. Stephen, each respectively holding and pointing towards the
instruments of their martyrdom—a grill and some stones. To enable
the worker to understand more clearly this rather unusual method of

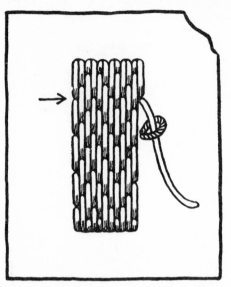

FIG. 233. MEDIÆVAL METHOD OF COUCHING.   FIG. 234. MEDIÆVAL METHOD OF COUCHING
                                                                    (REVERSE SIDE).

couching, a diagram of both sides of the work has been made, for an important part of the working lies at the back. (See also Plate XXXIII.)
It must be worked in a frame, and a fine, closely-woven linen should be
chosen for the ground. Some-
times, to increase its strength, a
twofold ground is used. To carry
out the work two needles must be
prepared, the one threaded with
strong linen thread and the other
with strands of silk or gold. The
two threads should be of about
the same thickness. After making
each thread secure at the back
bring the silk one through to the
surface at the top left-hand corner
of the form to be filled. Next
bring the linen thread through to
the surface about one-eighth of an
inch below (see arrow in diagram).

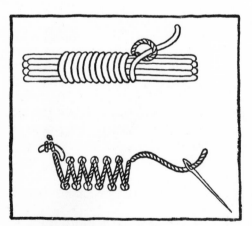

FIG. 235. COUCHED RAISED BAND.

Let it encircle the silk thread and then return to the back by the exact hole
through which it entered. It should pull through the silk thread with it
as it passes to the back. The silk during the process must be held rather
tautly by the left hand. For this stage of the working the right hand is

underneath the frame, pulling the linen thread through, and the left one above it holding firmly the silk thread, for unless there is some tension, too much of the silk will be taken through; only just as much should pass through as will cling closely round the linen thread at the back (see arrow in figure 234). This process repeated at correct intervals works the couching. Study of the two diagrams shows that on the surface the silk thread travels alternately up and down the form, and at regular intervals dips through to the back, and on the reverse side the linen thread passes in the same way down and up, following always the lead of the surface thread, and at regular intervals this surface thread is seen to encircle it. It is a curious coincidence that the method is

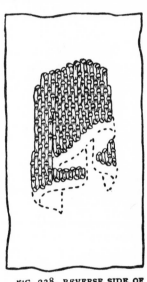

FIG. 236. TWO PATTERNS FOR COUCHING GOLD BY THE MEDIÆVAL METHOD OF WORK.

FIG. 237. FRAGMENT OF DRAPERY FROM A MEDIÆVAL VESTMENT.

FIG. 238. REVERSE SIDE OF DRAPERY.

identical with that of the lockstitch sewing machine.[1] With this form of couching, geometrical patterns are easily displayed upon the surface, for the linen thread always pulls the surface thread through to the back in some prearranged sequence, and this breaks up the surface into pattern. In the diagram a simple chevron pattern is in process of formation. It will at once be seen, that by varying the points at which the linen thread pulls the surface one to the back, other patterns could easily be displayed. (See figure 236.) In the ancient work, marvellously intricate and beautiful patterns were developed by this means of couching, such as repeating geometrical forms with heraldic figures occurring in the spaces between the interlacements. To execute patterns of this more complicated nature the couching has to be taken both horizontally and vertically, in one direction for the pattern and in the other for its background. The result gained is that of a rich damask, the play of light upon gold thread treated in this fashion is very effective.

[1] This was pointed out to the writer by M. Louis de Farcy, who writes at length upon this method of couching in *La Broderie du onzième siècle jusqu'à nos jours.*

Worked in silk thread this couching is easy to master, but in metal thread it is troublesome at first. There is often difficulty in obtaining really suitable gold thread. Japanese, in the usual form, is not practical, so it must be real gold thread of fine quality, otherwise it will not be sufficiently pliable. Working this couching in metal threads had better, perhaps, be

FIG. 239. A FRAGMENT OF AN ENGLISH MEDIÆVAL VESTMENT, S. LAWRENCE AND S. STEPHEN.

left to the professional worker, but in silk an amateur may attempt it with hope of almost immediate success. Some find a light tracing of the pattern over the ground a help, others prefer to work by the thread of the fabric, or by the guidance of the line before. Unnecessary difficulties may be encountered by not using correct materials. Needles and threads must be of suitable size in order not to make too large or too small a hole in the ground fabric, and for the same reason the linen must be closely woven and firmly stretched in the frame. The stitches must be straight, flat, and lie closely beside each other and carry out the pattern with mathematical accuracy, for no geometrical pattern looks well otherwise.

PLATE XXXIV. *Couched Knots on a Decorated Ground. Broad Borders in Diamond stitch. Outer and Inner Border in Coral.*

PLATE XXXV. APPLIED EMBROIDERY. In Buff, Grey and White Linens on a Black Linen Ground. Edged with Natural-coloured Tape, couched down with Orange and Black Threads.

The angle of the chevron, or whatever pattern it is, must be acute or the result will not be satisfactory. The same method of couching is employed to work the raised band illustrated in figure 235. This is a neater and stronger method of covering a padded line with thread than the modern one of couching the threads down upon the surface. The difference between the two methods is very slight, for instead of a tie down on the surface of the material the thread is pulled just through to the back. The lower part of the diagram gives the appearance at the back, and the upper shows the raised band. At the back of the linen the couching thread runs to and fro in zigzag fashion, pulling the couched thread only just through, and it is done in the same manner as for the filling in figure 233—that is, by the linen thread entering and returning through the same hole and pulling the surface thread with it. The advantages of this method of couching a raised band will be seen at once. Instead of a clumsy turning round of the laid thread on the surface at the point where it is secured by the couching thread, the turn is neatly hidden at the back. And it is a more durable method than the other for the tying down thread, because unseen, can be much thicker, also it is exposed to no friction. Although embroidery is by no means only a matter of stitches and methods of work, the importance of technique must always be insisted upon. It is shown in the present instance. Without the aid of this form of couching English needlework in the thirteenth century could not have reached the perfection that it did. There is no doubt that this ingeniously devised method of couching the gold thread, though it was not confined to use in England, had its share in making the fame of our world-renowned mediæval embroidery known as Opus Anglicanum.

CHAPTER XII—APPLIED AND INLAID WORK—QUILTING

APPLIED embroidery, also known as *appliqué*, includes all work in which the design is cut out of one material, laid upon another, and secured to it by stitching round the margins. The second material thus forms the background to the design. Sometimes the applied parts are previously enriched with embroidery, but more often than not they are merely silhouettes shaped in plain fabric. By the closely allied method called ' inlaid work,' both design and background are cut from different stuffs, and the intersecting parts, in appearance similar to a jig-saw puzzle, are sewn down upon a foundation material concealed beneath them.

Both methods go back to ancient times. The funeral tent of Queen Isiemkheb (*circa* 980 B.C.), preserved in the Cairo Museum, is an early example. Its rich design is built up with hundreds of pieces of gazelle hide, dyed in various hues, skilfully joined together at the edges. The Latin term ' opus consutum,' repeated several times in an Inventory of the vestments belonging to St. Paul's Cathedral drawn up in A.D. 1295, is thought to refer to work of this kind. The embroidered angels and formal sprigs (figure 240) that were commonly powdered over the surfaces of fifteenth- and sixteenth-century English copes and chasubles, were worked independently upon linen grounds in gold threads and coloured silks, and afterwards applied to the velvet grounds used for vestments during that period. It was then customary to embroider some additional light scrolling decoration directly upon the velvet ground surrounding the applied elements, a device that masked the joins and prevented them appearing detached from the context. Embroidery always has a more satisfactory appearance when it is executed directly upon the material that forms its background ; but when ground fabrics such as velvet are used, the direct method demands great skill in manipulation.

As applied and inlaid work are most effective when seen from a distance, these methods are particularly suitable for use in decorating things such as hangings, banners, and lecterns or altar frontals. But if the design is appropriate to the bold treatment required, there are many other purposes to which the two methods may be put. It is

PLATE XXXVI. INLAID EMBROIDERY. In Black and Stone-coloured Linens. The Marginal Lines of the Pattern in Striped Woven Band Stitch.

PLATE XXXVII. QUILTING. *In Back Stitch in Sepia and Fawn-tinted Silks upon Cream-coloured Linen.*

essential that the designs should be more or less formal, and be made up of elements having clear, simple outlines. Knotwork and counterchange patterns are eminently suitable (see Plates XXXV and XXXVI), and foliage and flowers, and birds and beasts lend themselves kindly to silhouette treatment if well posed and drawn with due formality (figure 241). Heraldry is so perfectly rendered by the two methods that they seem almost to have been invented for it. On the other hand, attempts at naturalistic representation should be avoided, as the finesse necessary for such work is technically impossible, and tends to incoherence.

Figured or plain fabrics, velvets, silks, and linens, are all suitable materials for working applied or inlaid embroideries. As, however, there is but little intrinsic interest in the technique employed, the colours and textures of the fabrics used become important factors in the design, and their choice calls for close attention. Materials that fray readily at the cut edges are troublesome to manipulate. If used, they may be lightly pasted at the back, along the margins ; an expedient sometimes essential, but to be avoided when possible, as it is tiresome to carry

FIG. 240. SPRIG FROM A FIFTEENTH-CENTURY ENGLISH ALTAR FRONTAL.

out successfully. The edges of the stuffs applied are either masked by couching upon them a cord, braid or hank of thread, or the cut margins are turned in, and then hemmed down. A remarkable example of applied work treated in this fashion is exhibited in the Real Armeria at Madrid, a magnificently decorated tent that was captured from Francis I at the battle of Pavia (1525). The predominant elements

FIG. 241. FRAGMENT OF A THIRTEENTH-CENTURY EMBROIDERED HANGING.

in its design are large leaf-shaped forms cut from silk and linen fabrics which are heavily enriched with formal flowers and foliage in tints of blue, scarlet, yellow and green.   In this piece no applied edging covers the securing stitchery; all the margins of the innumerable elements are turned in and hemmed to the natural-coloured linen foundation.

It is, however, more usual to complete the margins of applied elements with some kind of edging braid.   This can be couched down with thread of a contrasting colour ; and the couching thread may, if desired, pattern the braid with crosses, or some other small decorative device (see figure 224).   An embroidery stitch, such as Buttonhole, is sometimes used as an edging.   Other stitches, not so familiar, but perhaps more suitable, are those included in the group worked on a previously laid foundation, such as the examples illustrated in figures 112–115. If stitches of this kind are used, the threads upon which they are worked fulfil a dual purpose, for they both secure the applied fabrics to their backgrounds, always an essential operation, and at the same time they provide a basis for the stitch.

The margins of the inlaid design shown in Plate XXXVI are executed in Striped Woven Band (figure 114), a composite stitch worked upon a close series of short parallel threads.   When a twisted cord is adopted as an edging it is usual to fix it down invisibly, by slightly untwisting the strands and inserting the needle in the interstice thus formed.   The choice of colour and tone of the edging is important, for if it resembles too closely either the applied fabric or the background it increases the area covered by one or other of them, a result that makes a considerable difference in the appearance of the composition when finished.

To execute applied embroidery, begin by tracing the design upon both the ground fabric and the fabrics to be attached to it.   The ground material should then be stretched, not too tautly, in a frame.   Next, cut out with sharp scissors the various elements composing the design, already traced on the materials to be applied.   Care must be taken to leave a narrow space outside the traced line, a necessary precaution as this part will later be covered by the edging band.   The next process is to fix the shaped elements in their places on the foundation fabric, securing them in position with small pins.   Then replace the pins by a light tacking with fine thread, taking care that the applied pieces lie perfectly flat, as the slightest wrinkle on their surfaces will spoil the effect of the completed work.   Next secure the applied elements firmly to the background by means of small stitches set round their margins, and placed at right angles to them.   The final task is to couch down the edging cord or braid, so as to hide the securing stitches, and give a pleasing finish to the whole composition.

Inlaid embroidery follows the same method of execution as applied work.   Inlaying, however, demands the nicest care in cutting out both the pattern and the ground, or the two parts will not fit accurately when laid in position, and it will be difficult to cover their junctions with the edging braid.   Counterchanging patterns are particularly suitable for inlaying, as interlocking designs of this type make it possible to use up such cut-out material as would otherwise be discarded in a companion piece of work, in which the relationship between the two inlaid fabrics is reversed ; the stuffs forming the ground and the pattern in the one becoming respectively the pattern and the ground in the other. This device not only economizes materials but also saves labour in cutting them out. By alternating splendid velvets and satins in counterchanges the Italian workers of the sixteenth century and later times produced magnificent wall-hangings, often many yards in length, enriched with recurring designs of remarkable intricacy.

QUILTING.—Quilting is a method of work by which two fabrics are firmly joined together, one above the other, by lines of stitching. More often than not a layer of some soft springy material is inserted between the surface and foundation stuffs, an addition that makes the interstices between the stitches to stand out in low relief. To raise quilting to the level of an art—it has purely practical uses—the structural stitchery must follow some pleasing design.

That quilting was practised in England during the Middle Ages is shown by contemporary inventories. One, detailing the goods belonging to Robert Hathbrand, Prior of the Monastery attached to Canterbury Cathedral (1339–1370) mentions ' unum quilte album cum duobus tapetis albis cum Griffonibus.' This kind of embroidery was very popular in the seventeenth and eighteenth centuries, and many exquisite examples dating from that period still exist. It was then used not only for coverlets, but also for costumes. Men wore quilted suits in the seventeenth century, and the women's satin petticoats and stomachers were enriched by the same means. Oriental workers have always excelled in this method of embroidery. It is probable that the various phases of its development in the West from medieval times onwards reflect recurring Oriental influences. English quilting executed towards the end of the seventeenth century shows very plainly how our growing intercourse with the East was then affecting such work. A beautiful example of Sicilian workmanship, dating from about A.D. 1400, now exhibited in the Victoria and Albert Museum, shows an earlier type of design used in quilting. The surface is covered with a series of scenes from the life of Tristan, drawn with great dramatic effect and masterly precision, mainly in outline with pale brown thread, upon a background formed of fairly close lines of running stitches in white thread. The interlayer of stuff inserted behind the scenes consists of stout wool padding, a treatment that makes the composition stand out boldly, leaving the parts beneath the background, padded more lightly, in lower relief.

Although designs may be wholly of quilting, the quilting is often used to execute a subsidiary background to floral ornament embroidered in coloured silks (see figure 242). When employed in this way, the quilted pattern usually takes the form of a diamond-shaped trellis, a repeating shell-shape, closely twisted scrolls, or meandering lines (see figure 243). More intricate patterns, based upon formal foliage or geometrical figures, are also used for the purpose.

FIG. 242. QUILTING USED AS A SUBSIDIARY BACKGROUND PATTERN TO FLORAL
ORNAMENT EMBROIDERED IN COLOURED SILKS.

Back, Run and Chain stitches are all used to execute quilted patterns (figures 26 and 53), the first two being most popular. When Chain is adopted, the design is sometimes stitched on the underside, a treatment that results in a Back stitch on the front. Fine silk, either white or tinted in various shades of gold, is the usual thread employed for

FIG. 243. EXAMPLES OF QUILTED BACKGROUND PATTERNS.

executing the pattern. The surface fabric is generally a finely woven soft linen, although certain silk materials are also suitable. The backing may be of any stuff that suits the size of the work and the purpose to which it is to be put. The interlayer must be of a springy substance; flannel is often appropriate, also cotton wool. A material called 'domett' is sold for the purpose; a fabric that makes an under-lining optional, although the omission of it results in less relief in the raised pattern. For some designs, particularly those in which narrow parallel lines frequently occur, the padded effect is obtained by inserting a soft cord after the stitching is completed. To introduce the cord for this form of padding, the lining, always an openly woven fabric, is pierced with a stiletto, and the cord threaded into place with the help of a blunt-pointed needle. At the end of the line the cord is brought out by the same means, and its entrance and exit closed up as far as possible by pushing the divided threads of the fabric back into place. If the pattern needs emphasis, a coloured cord may be inserted ; a treatment that will lightly tint the surface to any required shade. A form of quilting now popular introduces variously tinted wools into different parts of the pattern. A finely woven shot silk makes an attractive surface material, and by working the quilting with black thread in Running stitch a definite outline is given to the coloured design. The colours of the padding wools must be very bright if they are to be effective when seen through the silk.

INDEX